The Wage Gap

Other Books in the Current Controversies Series

The Wage Gap

Noël Merino, Book Editor

GREENHAVEN PRESS
A part of Gale, Cengage Learning

GALE
CENGAGE Learning·

Farmington Hills, Mich • San Francisco • New York • Waterville, Maine
Meriden, Conn • Mason, Ohio • Chicago

GALE
CENGAGE Learning·

Elizabeth Des Chenes, *Director, Content Strategy*
Douglas Dentino, *Manager, New Product*

© 2014 Greenhaven Press, a part of Gale, Cengage Learning

WCN: 01-100-101

Gale and Greenhaven Press are registered trademarks used herein under license.

For more information, contact:
Greenhaven Press
27500 Drake Rd.
Farmington Hills, MI 48331-3535
Or you can visit our Internet site at gale.cengage.com

For product information and technology assistance, contact us at

Gale Customer Support, 1-800-877-4253
For permission to use material from this text or product, submit all requests online at www.cengage.com/permissions

Further permissions questions can be emailed to permissionrequest@cengage.com

Articles in Greenhaven Press anthologies are often edited for length to meet page require-ments. In addition, original titles of these works are changed to clearly present the main thesis and to explicitly indicate the author's opinion. Every effort is made to ensure that Greenhaven Press accurately reflects the original intent of the authors. Every effort has been made to trace the owners of copyrighted material.

Cover image © Jenny Matthews/In Pictures/Corbis.

LIBRARY OF CONGRESS CATALOGING-IN-PUBLICATION DATA

The wage gap / Noël Merino, book editor.
    pages cm. -- (Current controversies)
    Includes bibliographical references and index.
    ISBN 978-0-7377-6892-3 (hardcover) -- ISBN 978-0-7377-6893-0 (pbk.)
    1. Pay equity--United States. 2. Equal pay for equal work--United States. 3. Dis-crimination in employment--United States. I. Merino, Noël.
    HD6061.2.U6W34 2014
    331.2'1530973--dc23

                                                                    2013045335

Printed in the United States of America
1 2 3 4 5 6 7 18 17 16 15 14

Contents

Chapter 1: Is the Wage Gap Between Men and Women Due to Discrimination?

The highly touted pay gap between men and women is a false myth. When wages of men and women within the same occupation are compared, the so-called gender gap virtually disappears. It is also untrue that women are discouraged from entering high-paying fields and that there is a glass ceiling preventing women from attaining the highest levels of corporate management. The fact is that women often choose to work in less demanding and more flexible jobs, leading to lower wages and fewer career advancements.

Between 1970 and 2010, income growth was greater for upper-income households than for middle- and lower-income households. The growth in wealth, as opposed to income, for upper-income families is even more pronounced, as that sector was the only one to see notable gains in wealth from 1983 to 2010; the net worth of lower- and middle-income families during this period is virtually unchanged.

Yes: The Wage Gap Between Rich and Poor Is Harmful

Median household income varies by race and Hispanic origin, with all groups having a lower median income in 2011 than prior to the recession of 2001. The greatest decline in median household income during this period was experienced by blacks (down 16.8 percent) and Hispanics (down 10.8 percent).

Yes: The Wage Gap Among Races Is Problematic for Society

While a college education for low-income students would be an effective tool to reduce income inequality, most colleges today—both public and private—are enrolling fewer low- and middle-income students because they cannot afford to. Instead, they have shifted dollars away from financial aid to fund other amenitites in order to attract full-pay, high-income students. As such, government action is needed to end these practices, so that colleges can help to eliminate economic inequality through education, not increase inequality through unaffordability.

No: Education Is Not Key to Reducing Wage Gaps

Getting more low- and middle-income people to attend and graduate from college will not reduce income inequality, as many experts claim. The fact is that the United States currently has an adequate supply of college graduates to meet the demand for jobs, and increasing the number of graduates will result in an oversupply and lower, not higher, wages. While college graduates will continue to fair better than those without college degrees, a four-year college education is not the cure to the wage gap many believe.

The money spent on a college degree does not always result in higher earnings, especially when spent at less selective schools and on certain fields of study. While evidence clearly shows that the return on a four-year college degree is highly positive, a bachelor's degree is not a smart investment for every student. For this reason, policy makers should take steps to ensure that parents and students have critical information and alternative options concerning education after high school.

Children that come from affluent families have inherent advantages over middle- and low-income households that only increase as they progress through life. As these inherited advantages reinforce each other and accumulate, they increase the barriers to upward mobility and success of less-fortunate families. While there are individuals who overcome their disadvantages and achieve prosperity, statistics consistently show that children born in the bottom quartiles of wealth, even those who manage to get a college degree, will remain there their entire lives. As such, government programs and investment are needed to minimize these wealth advantages and expand the mobility of all Americans.

Foreword

By definition, controversies are "discussions of questions in which opposing opinions clash" (*Webster's Twentieth Century Dictionary Unabridged*). Few would deny that controversies are a pervasive part of the human condition and exist on virtually every level of human enterprise. Controversies transpire between individuals and among groups, within nations and between nations. Controversies supply the grist necessary for progress by providing challenges and challengers to the status quo. They also create atmospheres where strife and warfare can flourish. A world without controversies would be a peaceful world; but it also would be, by and large, static and prosaic.

The Series' Purpose

The purpose of the Current Controversies series is to explore many of the social, political, and economic controversies dominating the national and international scenes today. Titles selected for inclusion in the series are highly focused and specific. For example, from the larger category of criminal justice, Current Controversies deals with specific topics such as police brutality, gun control, white collar crime, and others. The debates in Current Controversies also are presented in a useful, timeless fashion. Articles and book excerpts included in each title are selected if they contribute valuable, long-range ideas to the overall debate. And wherever possible, current information is enhanced with historical documents and other relevant materials. Thus, while individual titles are current in focus, every effort is made to ensure that they will not become quickly outdated. Books in the Current Controversies series will remain important resources for librarians, teachers, and students for many years.

In addition to keeping the titles focused and specific, great care is taken in the editorial format of each book in the series. Book introductions and chapter prefaces are offered to provide background material for readers. Chapters are organized around several key questions that are answered with diverse opinions representing all points on the political spectrum. Materials in each chapter include opinions in which authors clearly disagree as well as alternative opinions in which authors may agree on a broader issue but disagree on the possible solutions. In this way, the content of each volume in Current Controversies mirrors the mosaic of opinions encountered in society. Readers will quickly realize that there are many viable answers to these complex issues. By questioning each author's conclusions, students and casual readers can begin to develop the critical thinking skills so important to evaluating opinionated material.

Current Controversies is also ideal for controlled research. Each anthology in the series is composed of primary sources taken from a wide gamut of informational categories including periodicals, newspapers, books, US and foreign government documents, and the publications of private and public organizations. Readers will find factual support for reports, debates, and research papers covering all areas of important issues. In addition, an annotated table of contents, an index, a book and periodical bibliography, and a list of organizations to contact are included in each book to expedite further research.

Perhaps more than ever before in history, people are confronted with diverse and contradictory information. During the Persian Gulf War, for example, the public was not only treated to minute-to-minute coverage of the war, it was also inundated with critiques of the coverage and countless analyses of the factors motivating US involvement. Being able to sort through the plethora of opinions accompanying today's major issues, and to draw one's own conclusions, can be a complicated and frustrating struggle. It is the editors' hope that Current Controversies will help readers with this struggle.

Introduction

"The question for society is whether particular wage gaps are justified or whether such gaps need to be remedied."

Wages vary widely among individuals in the United States. In 2012, the federal minimum wage was $7.25 per hour, so that a worker making minimum wage and working full time would have an annual wage of just over $15,000. At the other end of the spectrum, *Forbes* reports that in 2012, at least a hundred chief executive officers made over $15 million. There is no doubt that there is a gap in pay between the least paid workers and the highest paid workers. The question for society is whether particular wage gaps are justified or whether such gaps need to be remedied. A recent court case illustrates some of the issues and controversies that surround the debate about differences in pay.

Lilly Ledbetter worked for Goodyear Tire & Rubber Company from 1979 to 1998. In her memoir, *Grace and Grit: My Fight for Equal Pay and Fairness at Goodyear and Beyond*, she writes about how she discovered in 1998 that several men in her same position who had also started in 1979 were all making more money than her:

> Someone had listed my name and those of the three other tire-room managers, with salaries next to each name.... Over the years, I'd worried about being paid less than the men who were doing the same work I was, but I didn't have any proof.... But now there it was in plain black ink, what I'd always feared: The other managers, all men, had been making more than I was.

Ledbetter filed formal charges with the Equal Employment Opportunity Commission (EEOC) and, after her early retirement later in 1998, filed a lawsuit in the district court charging pay discrimination under Title VII of the Civil Rights Act of 1964 and the Equal Pay Act of 1963. The court ruled in favor of Ledbetter, awarding back pay and damages.

Goodyear appealed the case arguing that back pay and damages beyond those going back 180 days prior to her EEOC filing were not due to Ledbetter since there was a statute of limitations on discrimination claims. The court of appeals agreed, and on final appeal to the US Supreme Court in 2007, that ruling was upheld. The Supreme Court decision prompted the passage, two years later, of the Lilly Ledbetter Fair Pay Act, which allows the 180-day statute of limitations to reset with each paycheck that is affected by past discrimination. The text of the Lilly Ledbetter Fair Pay Act notes, "The limitation imposed by the Court on the filing of discriminatory compensation claims ignores the reality of wage discrimination and is at odds with the robust application of the civil rights laws that Congress intended."

Several controversial issues were raised by the Ledbetter case and resulting legislation. In order for a difference in pay to be legally egregious, it must be proven that the gap is caused by discrimination based on sex, race, ethnicity, religion, or national origin. On the one hand, since proving this requires access to witnesses and records, there is an argument to be made to have a statute of limitations. Legal journalist Stuart Taylor Jr. writes,

> The longer the wait, the more difficult it will be for the employer to contest an employee's one-sided and perhaps false account of the case, because key witnesses may have retired or died and records such as performance evaluations may have been discarded.

> Indeed, some of the Ledbetter law's vague language could be construed as opening the doors for people to sue a company even years after retiring, on the theory that each new pen-

sion check is too small because of some claim of discrimination by some long-since-departed (or dead) supervisor.

Differences in pay may or may not be an indication of discrimination, so assessing the issue necessitates looking at the evidence. On the other hand, giving people longer to file discrimination suits puts more pressure on employers to ensure pay is equal. President Barack Obama remarked after the act's signing:

> This bill is an important step—a simple fix to ensure fundamental fairness to American workers. . . . I know that if we stay focused, as Lilly did—and keep standing for what's right, as Lilly did—we will close that pay gap and ensure that our daughters have the same rights, the same chances, and the same freedom to pursue their dreams as our sons.

Like President Obama, many see the passage of the act as an important part of closing the gap in pay between men and women. Still others contend that more legislation is needed to ensure equal pay for all. Bryce Covert, economic policy editor for the progressive blogging site ThinkProgress, claims that the Lilly Ledbetter Fair Pay Act is "a baby step forward in the march toward equal pay." The National Organization for Women (NOW) argues that Congress should pass the Paycheck Fairness Act, which would require stronger proof from employers showing differences in pay are not discriminatory and would strengthen penalties for equal pay violations. According to NOW it also would

> deter wage discrimination by prohibiting retaliation against workers who inquire about employers' wage-practices or disclose their own wages. . . . This non-retaliation provision would have been particularly helpful to Lilly Ledbetter, because Goodyear prohibited employees from discussing or sharing their wages. This policy delayed her discovery of the discrimination by more than a decade.

But critics of this proposed legislation, such as The Heritage Foundation, argue that the new law "would mean millions of dollars for trial lawyers but fewer jobs for most Americans."

There is no shortage of controversies in discussing pay gaps. The issue of whether or not such gaps are problematic and the question of what to do about them have a variety of responses. By presenting different points of view on this issue, *Current Controversies: The Wage Gap* helps to shed light on this timely social issue.

Is the Wage Gap Between Men and Women Due to Discrimination?

Overview: Women's Earnings

Bureau of Labor Statistics, US Department of Labor

The Bureau of Labor Statistics is an agency within the US Department of Labor that is responsible for measuring labor market activity, working conditions, trends in US wages, and price changes in the economy.

In 2011, women who were full-time wage and salary workers had median usual weekly earnings of $684, about 82 percent of median earnings for male full-time wage and salary workers ($832). In 1979, the first year for which comparable earnings data are available, women earned 62 percent of what men earned.

This report presents earnings data from the Current Population Survey (CPS), a national monthly survey of approximately 60,000 households conducted by the U.S. Census Bureau for the U.S. Bureau of Labor Statistics (BLS). Information on earnings is collected from one-fourth of the CPS sample each month. Readers should note that the comparisons of earnings in this report are on a broad level and do not control for many factors that can be significant in explaining earnings differences. . . .

Earnings and Age

Median weekly earnings were highest for women age 35 to 64 in 2011, with little difference in the earnings of 35- to 44-year-olds ($734), 45- to 54-year-olds ($744), and 55- to 64-year-olds ($749). Among men, those age 45 to 64 had the highest earnings, with 45- to 54-year-olds ($979) having made about the same as 55- to 64-year-olds ($997). Young women and men age 16 to 24 had the lowest earnings ($421 and $455, respectively).

Bureau of Labor Statistics, US Department of Labor, "Highlights of Women's Earnings in 2011," Report 1038, October 2012, pp. 1–3.

Among the age groupings of those 35 years and older, women had earnings that ranged from 75 percent to 81 percent of those of their male counterparts. Among younger workers, the earnings differences between women and men were not as great. Women earned 92 percent of what men earned among workers 25 to 34 years old and 93 percent as much as men among 16- to 24-year-olds.

Between 1979 and 2011, women's-to-men's earnings ratios rose for most age groups. Among 25- to 34-year-olds, for example, the ratio grew from 68 percent in 1979 to 92 percent in 2011, and the ratio for 45- to 54-year-olds increased from 57 percent to 76 percent.

The Variation by Race

Asian women and men earned more than their White, Black, and Hispanic or Latino counterparts in 2011. Among women, Whites ($703) earned 94 percent as much as Asians ($751), while Blacks ($595) and Hispanics ($518) earned 79 percent and 69 percent as much, respectively. In comparison, White men ($856) earned 88 percent as much as Asian men ($970); Black men ($653) earned 67 percent as much; and Hispanic men ($571), 59 percent.

Median weekly earnings vary significantly by level of educational attainment.

Earnings differences between women and men were widest for Whites and for Asians. White women earned 82 percent as much as their male counterparts in 2011, while Asian women earned 77 percent as much as their male counterparts. In comparison, both Black and Hispanic women had median earnings that were 91 percent of those of their male counterparts.

Across the major race and Hispanic ethnicity categories, women's inflation-adjusted, or constant-dollar, earnings have risen significantly since 1979. Earnings growth has been sharpest for White women, outpacing that of their Black and Hispanic counterparts. Between 1979 and 2011, inflation-adjusted earnings for White women rose by 32 percent, compared with an increase of 22 percent for Black women and 14 percent for Hispanic women. In contrast, earnings for White and Black men in 2011 were about the same as in 1979, after adjusting for inflation, while Hispanic men's earnings were down by 10 percent from their 1979 constant-dollar level. Asians were not included in this analysis because comparable data are not available back to 1979.

The Impact of Education

Median weekly earnings vary significantly by level of educational attainment. Among both women and men age 25 and older, the weekly earnings of those without a high school diploma ($395 for women and $488 for men) were about two-fifths of those with a bachelor's degree or higher ($998 for women and $1,332 for men) in 2011. Women and men with a high school diploma who had not attended college earned a little more than half of what women and men with a bachelor's degree or higher did, and those with some college or an associate's degree earned around two-thirds as much.

At each level of education, women have fared better than men with respect to earnings growth. Although both women and men without a high school diploma have experienced declines in inflation-adjusted earnings since 1979, the drop for women was significantly less than that for men: a 10-percent decrease for women—as opposed to a 33-percent decline for men. On an inflation-adjusted basis, earnings for women with a college degree have increased by 31 percent since 1979, while those of male college graduates have risen by 16 percent.

The Impact of Occupation

Women working full time in management, business, and financial operations jobs had median weekly earnings of $977 in 2011, which is more than women earned in any other major occupational category. Within management, business, and financial operations occupations, women who were chief executives and computer and information systems managers had the highest median weekly earnings ($1,464 and $1,543, respectively). The second highest paying job group for women was professional and related occupations, in which their median weekly earnings were $919. Within professional and related occupations, women who were lawyers ($1,631), pharmacists ($1,898), and physicians ($1,527) had the highest earnings.

The occupational distributions of female and male full-time workers differ significantly. Compared with men, relatively few women work in construction, production, or transportation occupations, and women are far more concentrated in administrative support jobs.

Women are more likely than men to work in professional and related occupations. Within this occupational category, though, the proportion of women employed in the higher paying job groups is much smaller than the proportion of men employed in them. In 2011, 8 percent of female professionals were employed in the relatively high-paying computer and engineering fields, compared with 44 percent of male professionals. Professional women were more likely to work in education and healthcare occupations, in which the pay is generally lower than that for computer and engineering jobs. Sixty-nine percent of female professionals worked in the education and healthcare fields in 2011, compared with 30 percent of male professionals.

Parenthood, Location, and Hours Worked

Of the 44.5 million women working full time in wage and salary jobs in 2011, a little more than one-third were mothers of children under age 18. Median weekly earnings for mothers of children under age 18 were $669. Earnings for women without children under 18 were $692.

Median weekly earnings and women's-to-men's earnings ratios vary by state of residence. The differences among the states reflect, in part, variation in the occupations and industries found in each state and in the age composition of each state's labor force. In general, the sampling error for the state estimates is considerably larger than it is for the national estimates; thus, comparisons of state estimates should be made with caution.

Unlike full-time workers, women and men who worked part time had similar median earnings.

Among full-time workers (that is, those working 35 hours or more per week in a job), men are more likely than women to have a longer workweek. Twenty-five percent of men, compared with 14 percent of women, worked 41 or more hours per week, in 2011. Women were more likely than men to work 35 to 39 hours per week: 13 percent as opposed to 5 percent. A large majority of both male and female full-time workers had a 40-hour workweek; among these workers, women earned 88 percent as much as men earned.

Earnings for Part-Time Employment

Women are more likely than men to work part time—that is, less than 35 hours per week on a sole, or principal, job. Women who worked part time made up 26 percent of all female wage and salary workers in 2011. In contrast, 13 percent of men in wage and salary jobs worked part time.

Unlike full-time workers, women and men who worked part time had similar median earnings. Median weekly earnings for female part-timers were $235 in 2011, little different than the $226 median for their male counterparts.

Among part-time workers, men tend to be younger than women. Forty-three percent of male part-time workers were 16 to 24 years old, compared with 28 percent of female part-time workers in 2011.

Earnings by the Hour

Sixty-two percent of women and 56 percent of men employed in wage and salary jobs were paid by the hour in 2011. Women who were paid hourly rates had median hourly earnings of $11.98, 87 percent of the median for men paid by the hour ($13.80).

In 2011, among workers who were paid hourly rates, 6 percent of women and 4 percent of men had hourly earnings at or below the prevailing federal minimum wage of $7.25.

Among both women and men, hourly paid workers age 16 to 19 were the most likely to have earnings at or below the minimum wage. Twenty-three percent of teenage workers paid hourly rates earned the prevailing federal minimum wage or less in 2011, compared with just 3 percent of hourly paid workers age 25 and older. Among 20- to 24-year-olds, 10 percent had earnings at or below the minimum wage.

Women's Wages Are Lower Due to Occupational Segregation

Ariane Hegewisch and Maxwell Matite

Ariane Hegewisch is study director and Maxwell Matite is a research intern at the Institute for Women's Policy Research.

Women's median earnings are lower than men's in nearly all occupations, whether they work in occupations predominantly done by women, occupations predominantly done by men, or occupations with a more even mix of men and women. During 2012, median weekly earnings for female full-time workers were $691, compared with $854 per week for men, a gender wage ratio of 80.9 percent. Added to the gender wage gap within occupations is the gender wage gap between occupations. Male-dominated occupations tend to pay more than female dominated occupations at similar skill levels, particularly in jobs that require higher educational levels. Tackling occupational segregation is an important part of eliminating the gender wage gap.

The gender wage gap and occupational segregation—men primarily working in occupations done by men, and women primarily working with other women—are persistent features of the U.S. labor market. Only four of the 20 most common occupations for men and the 20 most common occupations for women overlap. Four out of ten women (39.6 percent) work in traditionally female occupations and between four and five out of ten male workers (43.7 percent) work in traditionally male occupations; only 6.0 percent of women work in

Ariane Hegewisch and Maxwell Matite, "The Gender Wage Gap by Occupation," Institute for Women's Policy Research, April 2013. Copyright © 2013 by The Institute for Women's Policy Research. All rights reserved. Reproduced by permission.

traditionally male occupations and only 4.8 percent of men in traditionally female occupations. . . .

The Most Common Occupations for Women

The three largest occupations—'secretaries and administrative assistants,' 'elementary and middle school teachers,' and 'registered nurses'—together employ more than 13 percent of all women. More than 40 percent of full-time female employees worked in only 20 occupations, but only 15 percent of full-time male employees work in these occupations. Ten of these occupations are female sex-typed, meaning at least three out of four workers are women.

Within the 20 most common occupations for women, median full-time weekly earnings for women range from $1,086 per week for 'registered nurses' to $368 per week for 'cashiers.' Women earn less than men (these calculations include full-time workers only) in each of these most common occupations for women; the gender wage gap is largest for 'retail salesperson,' with a gender median earnings ratio for full-time work of 64.3 percent. Among all occupations with earnings for full-time workers, the gender gap is largest for 'insurance sales agents.' In two of the most common occupations, 'office clerks, general' and 'social workers,' women earn almost as much as men, with a wage gap of less than two percent. . . .

The 20 most common occupations for full-time working men . . . employ close to a third of male and one in seven female full-time workers; nine of the occupations are non-traditional for women, and in four out of the 20—'automotive service technicians and mechanics,' 'carpenters,' 'construction laborers,' and 'grounds maintenance worker'—there are too few women workers to estimate median weekly earnings for women.

Median full-time weekly earnings for men range from $2,275 for 'chief executives' to $403 for 'cooks.' Six of the most common 20 occupations have weekly earnings above $1,000, compared with only two of the most common occupations for women. Without exception, women's median earnings are less than men's in the 20 most common male occupations.

More than three times as many women (4.87 million) than men (1.24 million) work in occupations with median earnings for full-time work below the federal poverty threshold for a family of four.

Occupations with Poverty Wages

Four of the most common occupations for women—'cashiers,' 'waiters and waitresses,' 'maids and household cleaners,' and 'retail salespersons'—and one of the most common occupations for men—'cooks'—have median earnings for a full week of work that provide less than 100 percent of the U.S. Department of Health and Human Services' federal poverty levels for a family of four. The poverty levels refer to annual earnings and translating them into weekly earnings assumes that a worker would be able to get full-time work for 52 weeks a year; this may not always be possible in these occupations, characterized by considerable fluctuations in demand for labor and, hence, unstable earning opportunities.

A further six of the most common female and eight of the most common male occupations provide median earnings of less than 150 percent of the poverty threshold. Workers in these occupations are potentially placed among the working poor, with earnings that are often too high to qualify for public supports but too low to attain economic security. With one exception ('retail sales persons'), median earnings are below or near poverty for both men and women in such low wage occupations. These include occupations such as 'teacher assistants' and 'nursing, psychiatric, and home health aides.'

Low earnings are a significant problem for both male and female workers. Yet overall more than three times as many

women (4.87 million) than men (1.24 million) work in occupations with median earnings for full-time work below the
federal poverty threshold for a family of four.

The Gender Wage Gap by Race and Ethnicity

The gender wage gap differs by race and ethnic background.
Hispanic/Latina women have the lowest median earnings, at
$521 per week or 54 percent of the median weekly earnings of
white men; black women have median weekly earnings of
$599 or 63 percent of median weekly earnings of white men
($748). Asians have the highest median weekly earnings, for
both men and women, and the highest levels of educational
attainment. The wage gaps for Asian women compared with
Asian men, and white women compared with white men are
larger than the wage gap for the whole population; the wage
gaps between black female and male workers and Latino male
and female workers are smaller. . . .

> *Our analysis of the 20 most common occupations shows
> that women's median earnings are lower than men's
> within most occupations.*

A third of Asian and white women, a quarter of black
women but fewer than one in five Hispanic women work in
'professional and related' occupations; black and Hispanic
women are approximately twice as likely to work in service
occupations than white women; Asian women are considerably less likely than other women to work in 'office and administrative support' occupations, and Hispanic women are
most likely to work in 'production, transportation and material moving' occupations.

With one exception (black women's median earnings are
the same as black men's in 'office and administrative support')
in each of the major occupational groupings men earn more

than women of the same race or ethnicity. The gender earnings gap is magnified by a race and ethnic earnings gap. For example, Hispanic women in management, business, and finance, earn only 86 percent of Hispanic men in these occupations, while Hispanic men earn only 69 percent of white men's earnings, and Hispanic women earn only 59 percent of white male managers. The median earnings of Hispanic women are lower than the federal poverty levels in four occupational groups: 'service occupations,' 'production, transportation, and material moving occupations,' 'sales and related occupations,' and 'natural resources, construction, and maintenance' occupations. These four occupational groups collectively employ five out of ten (48.6 percent) Hispanic full-time women workers.

Fifty years after the Equal Pay Act of 1963 and almost fifty years after Title VII of the Civil Rights Act of 1964 made compensation discrimination illegal, a gender earnings gap remains. Our analysis of the 20 most common occupations shows that women's median earnings are lower than men's within most occupations, and that female-dominated occupations tend to have lower median earnings than male-dominated occupations. This has a particularly pernicious impact on the women who work in the lowest paid female occupations in 'nursing, psychiatric, and home health aides' and 'cleaning and housekeeping,' where even full-time work may leave them with earnings at or only marginally above the federal poverty threshold. Such poverty wages are particularly common for Latina women. The comparisons of earnings in broad occupational groups by race and ethnicity show that Latina women are particularly likely to be in the lowest paid jobs, even in the lower skilled occupations. Women and then families need enhanced efforts to ensure non-discriminatory hiring and pay practices, better training and career counseling, and work family supports.

Institutional Bias Partially Explains the Gender Wage Gap

Bryce Covert

Bryce Covert is the economic policy editor for ThinkProgress, a progressive blogging website of the Center for American Progress Action Fund.

The gender wage gap drew a spotlight in the [2012] presidential campaign, as both sides duked it out for women's votes. But while we accept the gap's persistence, we're still guessing at its origins. One explanation, from both the right and the left, is that women are less ambitious—either they make explicit choices to put family before work or they shrink from the opportunity to demand a higher salary or better job. This explanation seeks to explain the fact that many women are stalled in middle management and make up a pitiful percentage of America's C-suite.

The Ambition of Men and Women

When researchers have studied the ambition gap, they've discovered something peculiar: It's not there. Women do ask for more. They just aren't rewarded for it.

The research organization Catalyst, for example, found that among MBA [master of business administration] grads on a traditional career track, women are even more likely than men to seek out skill-building experiences and training opportunities and to make their achievements visible by asking for feedback and promotions. Women also reported similar rates of negotiating as men: 47 percent of women and 52 percent of men had asked for a higher salary during the hiring process, and 14 percent of women and 15 percent of men had asked for a higher position. No gap there.

A recent paper from the National Bureau of Economic Research reported similar findings. When it was not made explicit that prospective employees could negotiate salary, men were more likely than women to haggle anyway. But once it was made explicit, women drove an even harder bargain than men. Does that reflect an ambition gap or an equal hunger for higher pay?

Another way at the problem is to look at job satisfaction. If women are less ambitious, we'd expect them to be about equally satisfied with their careers as their male colleagues. But Catalyst found that men at all levels are *more* satisfied with their careers than women. Thirty-seven percent of men were very satisfied, compared to just 30 percent of women. The only place where men and women were equally dissatisfied was at the lowest rungs of a firm.

Even among extraordinarily ambitious and successful workers of both genders . . . research found a [wage] gap. . . . Twice as many of the most proactive men advanced to a senior executive level as similar women.

Same Ambition, Less Pay

What does become clear when researchers look at this problem is that women aren't rewarded for their ambition. Catalyst has spent extensive time evaluating this issue. Its first report followed recent MBA graduates—the "best and the brightest," in its own terms—to see how men and women fared.

Women's first jobs out of school were at a lower level than men, and men had higher starting salaries, even when the number of years of experience, time since the MBA, industry, and geography were taken into account. Maybe men just start off more ambitious?

But they don't. The findings held true even among men and women who aspired to the CEO [chief executive officer] or senior executive level. It also held true for men and women who didn't have children. It's not the mommy track. It's something else.

What's that something else? Is it choice of major? Choice of occupation? Early-life family requirements? It seems not. A recent study from AAUW [American Association of University Women] looked at men and women one year out of college and found a 7% gender earnings gap, even when school selectivity, grades, choice of major, choice of occupation, and hours-worked were taken into account.

Even among extraordinarily ambitious and successful workers of both genders, Catalyst research found a gap. They followed full-time workers who didn't take breaks for education or family reasons or self employment. The mommy-trackers were left out. But the gap didn't go away: Twice as many of the most proactive men advanced to a senior executive level as similar women. The report concludes, "[W]hen women used the same career advancement strategies as men, they advanced less."

What Holds Women Back?

Catalyst's most recent report may shed some light on part of what holds women back: They aren't given the highly visible assignments that are critical to helping employees advance.

Following the same group of high potentials, the study found that women are perhaps even more anxious to take on these big-time assignments, having more project-based experience than men. Men and women were also equally quick to jump on these opportunities. They both led projects about 18 months after getting their MBAs. Yet men were given larger and more critical projects, with twice the budget of women's projects, three times as many employees, more visibility to the boss, and a higher level of risk. Women were also given less international experience, even though men are just as likely to turn down these assignments.

There are institutional blocks to women asking for higher pay. A human resources company recently analyzed data from 20,000 companies and found that more women than men received raises—7.4 percent to 6.2 percent—cutting against the idea that women aren't sitting down to negotiate salary. But men got the bigger raises, snagging 60% of the extra money.

Choices aren't the only thing holding back women's earnings. Bias is happening, too, even if it's uncomfortable to call it out.

Who do we blame for the wage gap, then? Maybe, the managers. One study told 184 managers that they would have a limited pot of money to hand out in raises to employees with identical skills and responsibilities. The managers that were told they'd have to negotiate gave men two-and-a-half times the amount in raises that they gave to women before anyone sat down. This meant that the men didn't even need to negotiate for higher pay, while women were already at a disadvantage when they tried to bargain up, because the rest of the money was assigned to their male peers.

Choices and Biases

The fact that there is probably institutional bias against women in the workplace doesn't rule out the fact that some competent women choose to reduce their income based on personal decisions, especially family-care. Many still choose to change their career trajectories, or to work less, in order to raise children, or take care of aging family members. A quarter of all working women are part-time, far more than men. That's changing as the number of men who are stay-at-home dads has more than doubled over the last decade, but we can't ignore the way that society shapes these women's "choices" by telling them that they are default caretakers without providing affordable, quality-care options or paid-time-off for having a new child or one that gets sick.

Assuming that women have themselves to blame for the wage gap is an easy conclusion, because it doesn't ask us to think [about] the treatment of women in the workplace. In fact, women show just as much enthusiasm for getting ahead as their male peers. Choices aren't the only thing holding back women's earnings. Bias is happening, too, even if it's uncomfortable to call it out.

The Gender Wage Gap Is a Myth

Diana Furchtgott-Roth

Diana Furchtgott-Roth is a contributing editor at RealClear Markets.com, a senior fellow at the Manhattan Institute, and a columnist for the Washington Examiner.

We hear it over and over again: the myth of the gender wage "gap."

Here's President Obama, speaking on June 4 [2012]: "And we've made progress. But we've got a lot more to do. Women still earn just 77 cents for every dollar a man earns."

An Obama campaign TV ad, entitled "First Law," which began airing June 21, showed the same 77 cent figure.

Just one problem—it isn't true. Here are three myths about the wage "gap."

Myth 1: Women get less pay for equal work. The spurious assertion that women are paid 77 cents for a man's wage dollar comes from comparing the earnings of all full-time men with those of all full-time women.

The comparison is bogus, for two reasons. First, it lumps together men and women who work different numbers of hours—any hours above 35 hours per week. On average, full-time women work fewer hours than full-time men, often because they prefer it.

When comparisons are made between men and women who work 40 hours per week, women make 87% of men's earnings, according to the Labor Department. For men and women who work 30 to 34 hours a week, women make more, 109% of men's earnings. Second, the gap claim averages for each gender earnings from many and disparate vocations. For example, it averages women who work as social workers with men who work as investment bankers; female elementary school teachers with male engineers; and male loggers with female administrative assistants.

For their own reasons, many women enter so-called "helping professions," such as nursing, teaching, elder care, health services, nutrition, social work. These occupations pay less than do some more dangerous and physically-demanding lines of work that attract more men—engineering, mining, operating construction machinery.

Legitimate comparisons look at men and women with the same job tenure in the same position at the same firm. If there's a big difference under those circumstances, there may be discrimination, giving women grounds to sue. Federal law forbids discrimination, and permits such suits.

When economists compare men and women in the same job with the same experience, the analysts find that they earn about the same. Studies by former Congressional Budget Office director June O'Neill, University of Chicago economics professor Marianne Bertrand, and the research firm Consad all found that women are paid practically the same as men.

President Obama says he's in favor of equal pay. Does he practice what he preaches? Not according to my calculations from 2012 pay data published by the White House. I found that women staffers there were paid 91 cents on a man's dollar—if one calculates the figure, incorrectly, based on simple averages by gender. This is presumably because female staffers in these offices were not as senior as male staffers, or they held different types of positions, just as in the workforce as a whole.

Myth 2: Women are discouraged from enrolling in higher-paying fields—science, technology, engineering, math. Not true. No one prevents women from taking the curricula they prefer to get ahead.

However, fewer women choose to major in engineering, chemistry, and physics. More choose to take English literature, communications, and gender studies. Graduates in these fields are usually paid less than in the sciences.

Data for degrees awarded show that women are scoring ahead of men. According to the National Center for Education Statistics' Digest of Education Statistics, women were projected to get 58% of masters and bachelor's degrees, and over half of PhD degrees for the 2011–2012 academic year.

One 2010 study found that while women represented 11% and 12% of university tenure-track applicants in electrical engineering and physics, they received 32% and 20% of job offers.

Data on the courses of undergraduate study which women choose reveal their vocational preferences. In 2010, the top five woman-heavy majors were family and consumer sciences/human sciences (88% female); library science (87%); health professions and related programs (85%); public administration and social service professions (82%); and education (80%).

The top four man-heavy majors are more highly paid but draw relatively few women. They were military technologies and applied sciences (4% female); transportation and materials moving (11%); engineering and engineering technologies (17%); computer and information sciences and support services (18%); and economics (30%).

Leah Loversky, a senior at Pomona College in California majoring in economics, told me that most economics majors on her campus are men. Last semester, in a 21-student class on game theory, she was one of two women. (She got an A minus.) "No one tried to discourage me from taking the course," she said. "In fact, my fellow economics majors all encouraged me to take it."

Women who prepare for science and engineering are well rewarded in a job market that traditionally has been male-dominated. One 2010 study found that while women represented 11% and 12% of university tenure-track applicants in electrical engineering and physics, they received 32% and 20% of job offers. They were more likely than male applicants to get hired when they applied. This shows that in the sciences, employers seek to remedy the traditional gender imbalance by seeking out bright women, who benefit from affirmative action.

Myth 3: A discriminatory "glass ceiling" restricts women to lower-paying jobs and careers and keeps them out of senior management and the corner office. Many women, even those with excellent academic credentials, prefer to work part-time in order to combine work and family. Family-friendly jobs with flexible hours pay less than jobs with longer, inflexible hours. (Some feminists contend that this is unjust, but that is a separate issue.)

It's not the "glass ceiling" that keeps women out of the corner office, it's a choice of how much time and effort to put into one's career. Many in the millennium generation (born after 1980) call it "work-life balance." For men and women, to make it to the corporate top requires countless hours of work and travel and too little time for family. That means missed birthdays, football and field hockey games, and school productions. Women seem to mind missing these events more than men.

Consider women at Yale Law School. In 2012, as it has done in many other years, Yale Law Women, an organization of female law students at Yale Law School, made a list of "Top Ten Law Firms," in categories particularly noted for family friendliness.

They picked firms that offered part-time and flex-time work, as well as generous parental leave. "One of the goals of the Top Ten list is to generate discussion about family-friendly policies at top law firms," Yale Law Women wrote on its website.

These are women who have the credentials to aim for the executive suite at major corporations, but some are planning for part-time and flex-time. There's no problem with those choices, but these same women shouldn't cry discrimination when they don't make it to the top.

Myths and realities—women and men grow up with them. Some myths teach us moral and ethical truths, and we are the richer for them. But when myths try to teach us something demonstrably false—such as women earning less than men for the same work—we are all the poorer. It is time to discard false myths about women.

The "Equal Pay Day" Myth

Carrie Lukas

Carrie Lukas is the managing director and director of policy for the Independent Women's Forum and a senior fellow at the Goldwater Institute.

This month [April 2012], feminist groups celebrate Equal Pay Day, a pseudo-holiday based on the idea that women are systematically underpaid, making only about three-quarters of every dollar a man makes for the same work. Women, they claim, have to work until April to make up for last year's "wage gap."

Americans appropriately recoil from the idea of a sexist economy that short-changes hard-working women. If it were true, it would be outrageous.

Fortunately, however, this commonly repeated claim is false. There is no evidence that women are routinely paid a fraction of what men make for the same work, or that discrimination drives statistical differences between men and women's earnings.

The Department of Labor statistic underlying the "wage gap" claim simply compares a full-time working man's median wages with those of a full-time working woman, ignoring the many factors that affect earnings, including number of hours worked, industry, years of experience, and education, to name but a few. When such information is taken into account, the wage gap shrinks, and in some cases even reverses.

Feminist groups disserve women by promoting the false idea that the U.S. workplace is overwhelmingly sexist. It encourages unnecessary meddling from the federal government, which could limit women's job opportunities and workplace flexibility, and discourages women from fully pursuing their ambitions.

Women are better off understanding that it's the decisions they make—not systematic sexism—that determine how much they earn.

The Real Causes of Earning Differences

Women are an increasingly prominent economic force. Today, 47 percent of workers are women. Women hold more than half of all managerial and professional positions. Given that women are also getting college and advanced degrees in greater numbers than men, and that many companies pay premiums for educated workers, we can expect women's earnings and economic power to increase for years to come.

Yet in spite of this, women still earn, on average, less than men do. The Department of Labor's Bureau of Labor Statistics reported in the fourth quarter of 2011 that the median full-time working woman made 81.6 percent of the wages of the median full-time working man. That's an increase in women's earnings, which have hovered between 75 and 80 percent of men's earnings for several decades, but still a significant difference.

Big government, feminist organizations and liberal politicians repeat this "wage gap" statistic, implying that discrimination is its cause. President Obama, for example, in his 2012 State of the Union address made the pronouncement that "women should earn equal pay for equal work," as if this remains an illusive goal.

Audiences hearing such statements may understandably assume that it's the norm for two coworkers, one male and one female, working in the same position, with similar responsibilities and backgrounds, to be paid very differently, with the woman making a fraction of her male coworker.

Yet the statistic that is the basis for the "wage gap" claim doesn't purport to compare two, similarly-situated coworkers. It's a simple comparison of the median earnings of full-time working men and women, ignoring the many factors that we know influence how much someone earns.

Women gravitate toward jobs with fewer risks, more comfortable conditions, regular hours, more personal fulfillment and greater flexibility.

Consider time worked. The Department of Labor's 2011 Time Use Survey shows that full-time working men work about 5 percent more time at work each day on the job. Both are "full-time" workers for wage gap calculations, but it's hardly a surprise that someone who works more also earns more.

Women and men also pursue work in different economic sectors. Men dominate fields like construction, manufacturing and trucking, while women cluster in service industries, teaching, health care and the social services.

While some feminists suggest that women are coerced into lower-paying job sectors, most women will instinctively recognize that other factors are at work. Women gravitate toward jobs with fewer risks, more comfortable conditions, regular hours, more personal fulfillment and greater flexibility. Simply put, many women—not all, but enough to have a big impact on statistics—trade higher pay for other desirable job characteristics.

Men, by contrast, often take jobs that involve physical labor, outdoor work, overnight shifts and dangerous conditions (which is also why men suffer the overwhelming majority of deaths in the workplace). They put up with these unpleasant factors so that they can earn more.

Children, unsurprisingly, have a big role to play in this. Women with children (and those anticipating having children) tend to trade pay for greater flexibility or time from work. Working mothers take more leave time, are less likely to travel or move for a job, and value regular hours. In contrast, men who have children tend to pursue higher paying jobs. They may work longer hours or take on unpleasant positions in order to bring in more money to support the family.

In his book, *Why Men Earn More: The Startling Truth Behind the Wage Gap*, Dr. Warren Farrell dissects the impact of the different decisions men and women often make, noting how even within specific industries, women tend to pursue lower-paying positions.

Those seeking to cast women as victims portray such trends as evidence of socialization that steers women toward more child-rearing and lower-pay, but as Dr. Farrell suggests, these trends could just as easily be viewed as evidence of men's hardship. Men feel pressure from society to maximize their earnings and sacrifice their own physical safety, comfort, time, and even dreams in pursuit of bigger paychecks.

The question of who is the real victim, however, is really outside the scope of this debate. The important conclusion is that it's the different decisions that men and women make about work that drive differences in earnings—not discrimination.

What Would Happen If There *Was* a Wage Gap

Imagine if women really were all paid three-quarters of what men make for the same work. Companies that hired all women would have a huge competitive advantage. They would be able to charge their customers significantly less than male-employing competitors, and drive those male-dominated companies out of business.

Accepting the idea of a true "wage gap" requires believing that American companies are so riddled with sexism that propping up the patriarchy and over-paying men are higher priorities than earning a profit. This simply doesn't make sense, and there is no evidence to suggest that American companies do have such counterproductive priorities.

Wage Gap Misconceptions Encourage Bad Policy Decisions

Politicians and feminist organizations that trumpet the wage gap statistic typically have an agenda in mind. They want Washington to be more involved in determining compensation levels. Their hope is that government bureaucrats can make private payment practices more "fair" to women.

Concentrating power over compensation decisions in Washington may be sold as a way to "solve" the wage gap, but women will pay a high price in fewer job opportunities and less workplace flexibility.

The Paycheck Fairness Act, for example, has been routinely introduced in Congress and is often billed as a way to address the wage gap during Equal Pay Day events. This legislation would make it easier for employees to sue for discrimination, make it more difficult for employers to defend themselves against those charges, and compel employers to report on compensation practices to Washington bureaucrats. The Department of Labor would then use the data collected to offer "guidelines" for best compensation practices. As a result, businesses would face costly new paperwork burdens and greater potential litigation costs.

While this would leave less money for hiring in general, businesses would have a particular disincentive from offering flexible working arrangements. Today a working mom may have the opportunity to accept reduced take-home pay in return for shorter hours that allow her to be home after school hours. Yet with increased Washington oversight, employers are likely to formalize pay scales and avoid such gray areas that open themselves up to questioning and potential legal action.

Concentrating power over compensation decisions in Washington may be sold as a way to "solve" the wage gap, but women will pay a high price in fewer job opportunities and less workplace flexibility. And all Americans can expect a less dynamic economy and slower economic growth as a result.

Helping Women Earn More

Certainly, bad companies and bad bosses who mistreat employees exist in the United States. There are already laws on the books that make discrimination illegal, and employees who are mistreated can and should pursue recourse.

However, feminist groups do women a disservice by promoting the idea that women are consistently paid a fraction of what men earn for equal work. Women convinced that ubiquitous discrimination plagues the economy may look at bosses and male colleagues with suspicion, rather than as potential partners with a joint interest in their success and advancement. They may be less likely to pursue greater responsibilities in their jobs, believing that they won't be properly compensated for their contributions anyway.

The assumption that sexism drives earnings also discourages women from considering how the decisions they make affect earnings. Dr. Farrell details how small changes in the number of hours worked and specialties chosen can have significant, lasting impact on earning potential.

That's good information for women to consider. They may not always opt to maximize earnings, but they should be aware of the tradeoffs. Some have speculated that women may be less likely to negotiate on salaries and for raises, which may contribute to lower pay. That's an important factor to consider and something that empowers women: Women should understand that they need to be their own best advocates, and parents can help encourage their daughters to feel comfortable in talking about money.

Ultimately, women are better off understanding that their actions will largely determine their earnings, rather than feeling like helpless victims of a sexist economy.

Sex, Workers: Gender Discrimination Does Not Explain the Male-Female Pay Gap

Andrew Biggs

Andrew Biggs is a resident scholar at the American Enterprise Institute.

President Obama recently urged the Senate to pass the Paycheck Fairness Act, which would make it easier for women to sue their employers for gender discrimination. The act is needed, Obama said in a written statement, because "even in 2010, women make only 77 cents for every dollar that men earn." The House passed the legislation in 2009, but the Senate has yet to act.

Whereas under current law, women who sue their employers must prove gender bias, the Paycheck Fairness Act would shift the burden to employers to show that gender pay differences are not caused by bias. A woman could allege bias even if her better-compensated male coworkers were better educated and more highly skilled, forcing the employer to show that those extra qualifications were necessary for the job. The bill also would automatically sign women up for class-action gender-discrimination suits.

In urging passage of the act, Vice President Joe Biden exhorted senators to "get on the right side of history." But that would put them on the wrong side of almost every piece of rigorous research on gender pay. Indeed, an academic-literature survey published by the Department of Labor in

2009 concluded that discrimination's role in creating the pay gap may be practically non existent. Even White House domestic-policy chief Valerie Jarrett implicitly admitted, in the *Washington Post*, that the gender pay gap may be smaller if we factor in education and experience levels. She didn't say how much smaller, but the truth is that the 23 percent gender pay gap shrinks significanfly—and perhaps disappears altogether—when one accounts for various differences between men and women.

Among never-married individuals without children, for example, the pay gap is actually negative—in this group, women earn more than men, because they have better educational qualifications.

Once women do marry and have children, they are more likely to opt for employment that accommodates childcare responsibilities. More women work part-time than men, and women are twice as likely to work in the nonprofit sector, which offers lower pay but more flexible work conditions. Women are also four times more likely to leave the workforce temporarily to care for children. This reduces seniority and job-specific skills and discourages employers from investing in female employees, who may not stay long enough for such investments to pay off.

Men tend to enter careers involving more physical risks and less job security. The 25 most dangerous jobs are all male-dominated, and unemployment has risen significantly more for men than for women in the current recession. Men demand and receive higher pay to compensate for these risks.

In addition, men's lower aversion to risk might help them negotiate harder for wages. The American Association of University Women reports that men are four times more likely to bargain when it comes to salary in a new job than women are.

There is also evidence that women prefer positions with more generous benefits relative to wages—which, again, are often found in the government and non-profit sectors. Thus the gap in total compensation may be smaller than the gap in salaries alone. Economists Eric Solberg and Teresa Laughlin of California State University found that factoring in benefits eliminated around nine percentage points of the pay gap, and concluded that "any measure of earnings that excludes fringe benefits may produce misleading results as to the existence, magnitude, consequence, and source of market discrimination."

When all of these factors are considered, the pay gap may vanish almost completely. A study by former Congressional Budget Office director June O'Neill and Baruch College economics professor Dave O'Neill showed that accounting for differences in male and female worker characteristics such as education, years of experience, and chosen occupation boosts the female/male pay ratio to between 92 and 99 percent. The remaining difference could be attributable to gender discrimination, but could also be due to factors that aren't easily observed and controlled for. And even if we take the low-end estimate of 92 percent and assume that the entire remaining gap is due to discrimination, we have eliminated two-thirds of the gap cited by the White House.

Women need more markets, more enterprise, and more opportunity, not more regulation and litigation.

Similarly, the 2009 Department of Labor study mentioned above, which both reviewed existing literature and conducted its own statistical analysis of the pay gap, reached "the unambiguous conclusion that the differences in the compensation of men and women are the result of a multitude of factors and that the raw wage gap should not be used as the basis to justify corrective action." Yet it is precisely this raw wage gap that the White House cites in support of the Paycheck Fairness Act.

Discrimination is unlikely to drive the gender pay gap because, as economist Gary Becker pointed out a half century ago, when one employer underpays his workers, competing businesses can earn windfall profits by luring them away. If Employer A pays women 77 cents on the dollar, Employer B can hire all Employer A's female workers at 78 cents on the dollar to replace his costlier male workers. This raises Employer B's profits, while Employer A must now pay full freight for employees. The Royal Swedish Academy of Sciences noted, in awarding Becker the Prize in Economics, that "discrimination thus tends to be economically detrimental not only to those who are discriminated against, but also to those who practice discrimination." As long as there is a critical mass of non-discriminating employers—and the growth of female-run businesses in recent decades and changes in social norms among males indicates there is—then employers' profit motives will narrow the pay gap to levels justifiable in terms of productivity. Ironically, while the Left assumes that businesses readily sacrifice worker safety and degrade the environment in search of profits, they nevertheless believe employers forgo profits simply to satisfy a misbegotten desire to discriminate.

Discrimination is odious, but it is not in employers' interests to discriminate and discrimination is not a major cause of overall male-female pay differences.

Even if some of the pay gap is due to discrimination, therefore, economic liberalization may be the key to reducing it. Because employers that discriminate lose profits relative to non-discriminating competitors, increased competition weeds out discrimination. Several studies have shown that as industries faced increased competition, through either deregulation or international trade, the gender pay gap shrank. And the pay gap is larger in monopoly markets without competition and smaller in start-ups and small businesses that must be productive in order to survive. Women need more markets, more enterprise, and more opportunity, not more regulation and litigation.

If as a society we wish to subsidize female earners, we can do so more efficiently through policy than lawsuits. For instance, relative to what it pays men, Social Security pays women additional benefits equal to around 3 percent of lifetime earnings, because of the progressivity of the benefit formula and the fact that women live longer. Thus, Social Security by itself effectively raises female wages by 3 percent relative to men's, erasing much or all of any discrimination-based pay gap. Other programs surely have similar effects.

And even if there is a small remaining pay gap due to true discrimination, it is an open question whether that problem is worth solving with legislation that opens the door to a multitude of costly law suits. In addition to harming job creation, the risk of a pay-gap lawsuit could make employers less willing to hire women, effectively increasing gender discrimination.

The point isn't that discrimination can't or doesn't exist. It's that the Left discusses the pay gap almost solely with reference to discrimination when it is explainable almost entirely without reference to discrimination. Discrimination is odious, but it is not in employers' interests to discriminate and discrimination is not a major cause of overall male-female pay differences. The administration's claims of a 23 percent gender pay gap are best viewed as an election-year effort to foster resentment among women, a voter group that supported Democrats in 2008 but has more recently shifted against them. The president's deliberate disregard of the research crosses the line into policy malpractice. If enacted, the Paycheck Fairness Act will impose costs on employers, the economy, and the women it is intended to help.

Is the Wage Gap Between Rich and Poor Harmful?

Overview: The Gap in Income Between Rich and Poor

Pew Social & Demographic Trends

The Pew Research Center's Social & Demographic Trends project studies behaviors and attitudes of Americans in key areas of their lives, including family, community, health, finance, work, and leisure.

The median real income of U.S. households has increased markedly since 1970. In 2010, the median household income in the U.S. was $59,127 (expressed in 2011 dollars and adjusted for household size). That was 32% higher than the median income of U.S. households in 1970 ($44,845).

Household Income from 1970 to 2010

The increase in household income was remarkably steady from 1970 to 2000, increasing 12% each in the 1970s, the 1980s and the 1990s. However, the median household income in 2010 was less than in 2000, falling from $63,277 in 2000 to $59,127 in 2010, or a drop of nearly 7%. That is the lingering aftermath of the 2001 recession, an economic slowdown that persisted through 2003 and the Great Recession of 2007–2009.

The overall gains in income were shared by households in all three income tiers, albeit not equally. For middle-income households, the median income increased from $51,932 in 1970 to $69,487 in 2010, a gain of 34%. Over this period, the median income of lower-income households increased from $17,853 to $23,063, or by 29%. For upper-income households, the median income rose 43%, from $112,651 in 1970 to $161,252 in 2010.

Households in all three income tiers lost ground from 2000 to 2010. The median income for middle-income households fell from $72,956 to $69,487; the median for lower-income households dropped from $25,164 to $23,063; and the median income for upper-income households slid from $171,679 to $161,252.

The Differences Across Income Groups

The overall trend in income growth masks some differences across the decades and income groups. In the 1970s, income growth was the strongest for lower- and middle-income households (13% each). Incomes for upper-income households increased 10% in the 1970s.

The pattern reversed in the 1980s with the strongest gains (18%) experienced by upper-income households. That was significantly greater than the 11% growth in the median income of middle-income households. It also was more than double the increase of 8% for lower-income households. This decade marked the beginning of a widening of the income gap.

Lower-income households were among the greatest beneficiaries of the economic expansion in the 1990s. Their median income in the 1990s increased by 15%, almost double the rate of increase in the previous decade. The growth in the incomes of middle-income households (12%) and upper-income households (18%) were virtually unchanged from the 1980s.

In the "lost decade," 2000 to 2010, previous gains in incomes for all three tiers of households eroded. In this decade, the median income of lower-income households decreased 8%, the income of middle-income households fell 5%, and the median income for upper-income households dropped 6%.

The Distribution of Aggregate Income

The distribution of U.S. aggregate household income shifted away from the middle and lower tiers to the upper-income tier from 1970 to 2010. This is the consequence of two trends: the higher rate of growth in the incomes of upper-tier households and the decreasing share of adults who live in middle-income households.

The net result of the trends in household incomes and the distribution of the adult population is a more uneven distribution of aggregate income in 2010 than what it was in 1970.

In 2010, upper-income households accounted for 46% of U.S. aggregate household income. Their share in aggregate income was more than double the share of adults (20%) living in those households. Middle-income households accounted for 45% of U.S. aggregate household income in 2010, less than the share of adults (51%) living in those households. Lower-income households had a 29% share in the adult population but accounted for only 9% of aggregate income.

In 1970, upper-income households accounted for 29% of aggregate income, middle-income households had a 62% share, and lower-income households accounted for 10% of aggregate income. For the middle, the share in income was about the same as the share in the adult population in 1970 (61%). Upper-income households accounted for 14% of the adult papulation in 1970, and lower-income households accounted for 25%.

Income Growth for US Households

From 1970 to 2010, the share of middle-income households in aggregate income fell more sharply (by 27%) than its share in the adult population (down 16%). In contrast, the share of upper-income households in aggregate income rose faster (by

60%) than its share in the adult population (up 44%). For lower-income households, the share in aggregate income fell moderately (6%), despite a 15% increase in their share of the adult population.

The net result of the trends in household incomes and the distribution of the adult population is a more uneven distribution of aggregate income in 2010 than what it was in 1970. The shift in the distribution is most pronounced in the 1980s and the 1990s. Those are the two decades in which income growth was more pronounced for upper-income households compared with the growth in the incomes of middle- and lower-income households.

Based on wealth, the distances between lower-, middle- and upper-income families are much greater than the differences in income. Moreover, the wealth gap has increased by much more than the income gap in the past three decades. The most striking finding is that only upper-income families have experienced notable gains in wealth from 1983 to 2010; the net worth of lower- and middle-income families is virtually unchanged. This is a consequence of the housing market crash in 2006 and the Great Recession, which have seemingly erased nearly all of the wealth gains experienced by lower- and middle-income families in the two decades prior to the start of the Great Recession.

Rising Income Inequality Adversely Affects Many Social Systems

Elizabeth McNichol et al.

In addition to Elizabeth McNichol, Douglas Hall, David Cooper, and Vincent Palacios contributed to the folloiwng viewpoint. McNichol is a senior fellow and Palacios is a research associate at the Center on Budget and Policy Priorities. Hall is director of the Economic Analysis and Research Network (EARN), and Cooper is an economic analyst at the Economic Policy Institute.

It is a basic American belief that hard work should pay off—that individuals who contribute to the nation's economic growth should reap the benefits of that growth. Over the past three decades, however, the benefits of economic growth have been skewed in favor of the wealthiest members of society. Rising income inequality not only raises basic issues of fairness but also adversely affects our economy and political system.

The Negative Effects of Income Inequality

A widening gulf between the richest Americans and those at the bottom or middle of the income scale can reduce social cohesion, trust in government and other institutions, and participation in the democratic process. For example, two-thirds of respondents to a recent Pew Research poll indicated that they believe that there are strong conflicts between the rich and the poor. Growing income inequality also has exacerbated discrepancies in political influence in federal, state, and local

Elizabeth McNichol, Douglas Hall, David Cooper, and Vincent Palacios, "Pulling Apart: A State-by-State Analysis of Income Trends," Center on Budget and Policy Priorities and Economic Policy Institute, November 15, 2012, pp. 41–49. Copyright © 2012 by Center on Budget and Policy Priorities and Economic Policy Institute. Reproduced by permission.

government—a particular problem given political candidates' heavy dependence on private contributions. For example, in the 2008 election, over 70 percent of funding for campaigns for the House of Representatives—which totaled $854 million—came from large donations (over $1,000) or Political Action Committees. This may have contributed to the increase in the number of Americans who feel that their elected officials do not care much about the views of ordinary citizens.

In addition, inequality has negative effects on the nation's health, housing, and education. As the divide grows between families at the top of the income scale and everyone else, the richest Americans have less contact with everyone else—and thus less familiarity with the problems that typical Americans face. Metropolitan areas with rising income inequality experienced rapid growth in residential segregation by income between 1970 and 2000, according to a 2007 Brookings Institution study.

Because school systems depend heavily on local funding, increased income disparities have led to increased disparities in the quality of schools. As wealthier families have moved to the suburbs, low-income families have become increasingly concentrated in areas with low housing values. The result is lower property tax collections to support schools and other services. That makes it harder for children in low-income families to acquire the skills they need to succeed.

Segregation by income also reduces support for state taxes, which comprise almost half of funding for elementary and secondary schools. An upper-income family living in the suburbs may have trouble understanding the extent of the problems of schools in low-income neighborhoods. Similarly, wealthy families who can afford private schools for their children can lose sight of the need to support public schools. As a result, support for the taxes necessary to finance government programs declines, even as the nation's overall ability to pay taxes rises. The failure to invest adequately in programs that educate children, meet the health and housing needs of families at all income levels, and support low-wage workers can dampen the future economic growth of individual states and of the nation.

There is also evidence that income inequality causes more direct harm to people in poverty. For example, a number of papers prepared for a conference on income inequality sponsored by the Federal Reserve Bank of New York found a link between higher levels of inequality and poor schools, substandard housing, and higher levels of crime.

Growing income inequality threatens to undermine efforts to move more families from welfare to work.

The Research on Inequality

The impact of inequality on public health has received considerable attention from researchers. A recent article [by Gary Burtless] summarized this research: "Demographers and public health researchers have found mounting though controversial evidence that greater inequality can boost mortality rates and contribute to poor health. Countries and communities with above-average inequality have higher mortality rates than countries or communities with comparable incomes and poverty rates but lower inequality." The United States has substantially greater inequality than nearly all other developed nations. A recent study found that children in states with higher income inequality were less well-off than those in states with a more even distribution of income.

In addition to the link to overall health, a recent paper that examined differences among countries and among U.S. states found a strong connection between income inequality and social problems such as mental illness, violence, drug abuse, and poor educational performance.

Growing income inequality also widens the gap between housing costs and what households—particularly renters with very low incomes—can afford to pay. High housing costs reduce the disposable income that families have to pay for other essentials, such as food, transportation, and medical care. They also contribute to housing instability and homelessness, which can have severe and enduring effects on families, particularly young children.

In addition, growing income inequality threatens to undermine efforts to move more families from welfare to work. When low-wage jobs do not pay enough to lift a family out of poverty and when the incomes of the poorest families grow only slowly or not at all, policies that encourage work cannot succeed.

The recent decline in the incomes of the poorest families is particularly disturbing. Research has shown that poverty in childhood has a long and harmful reach. Even modest changes in family income for young children in poor families significantly affect their educational success—and may have a big effect on their earnings as adults. Poverty researchers Greg J. Duncan of the University of California, Irvine, and Katherine Magnuson of the University of Wisconsin found that children in low-income families that received an income boost when the children were under age 6 earned more and worked more as adults.

The Growing Wage Gap

The growth of income inequality in nearly every state mainly reflects two factors. The first is that the distribution of labor income (wages and salaries) is becoming increasingly unequal; in other words, the gap between high-wage and low-wage jobs is growing. The second is that investment income has grown faster than wage income. A combination of broad economic trends and state and national government policies has contributed to both of these developments.

The growing wage gap is the primary cause of the growth in income inequality. Wages are a key factor because they constitute about three-fourths of total family income. Wages at the bottom and middle of the wage scale have been stagnant or have declined over much of the last three decades. The wages of the very highest-paid employees, however, have grown significantly.

Wages have eroded for workers at the bottom and middle of the income scale for several reasons, as explained below.

The Availability of Jobs

One factor that affects wages is the supply of workers relative to the number of jobs available. When jobs are available but there are relatively few workers, employers must pay higher wages to fill job openings. The unemployment rate is one measure of the supply of workers; a high unemployment rate means that employers will have an easier time of finding workers, so there is less pressure on them to increase wages. The unemployment rate was higher on average over the last three decades than between the 1940s and the late 1970s. As a result, middle- and low-income workers have generally had much less bargaining power than in that earlier period.

The economy's shift from manufacturing to services has led to an increase in the number of low-paying jobs and a decline in higher-paying jobs for workers with less than a college education.

The one significant exception to the trend of growing wage inequality highlights the importance of full employment. The later part of the 1990s, a time of broadly shared growth in wages, was also a time of persistent low unemployment. That, plus an increase in the minimum wage, an expansion of the earned income tax credit, and rapid productivity growth, fueled real wage gains at the bottom and middle of the income scale.

Unemployment rates vary significantly from region to region. In 2011, when the national rate averaged 8.9 percent, state unemployment rates ranged from 3.5 percent in North Dakota to 13.5 percent in Nevada. The particular mix of industries in a state and changes in their fortunes can have a large effect on the relative level of inequality and growth in inequality in that state.

International trade also plays an important role in rising wage inequality. As U.S. imports have grown, the number of higher-wage manufacturing jobs available to non-college-educated workers has declined. In addition, workers in the United States may agree to wage concessions in response to employers' threats of moving production facilities to other countries. Research has generally found that the growth in imports has played an important role in the decline in relative earnings of non-college-educated workers and can explain about 15 percent to 25 percent of rising wage inequality. The effect may be growing. There is also some recent evidence that expanded trade with very low-wage countries such as China has increased the inequality-inducing impact of international trade.

Changes in the U.S. Economy

Several other fundamental changes in the U.S. economy have also helped widen the wage gap. The economy's shift from manufacturing to services has led to an increase in the number of low-paying jobs and a decline in higher-paying jobs for workers with less than a college education. Between 1979 and 2011, employment in manufacturing fell from 22 percent of all U.S. jobs to 9 percent, while employment in service industries rose from 72 percent of jobs to 86 percent. Many service-sector jobs are lower paid than comparable manufacturing jobs; between 2008 and 2010, for example, average weekly earnings for an employee working in non-manufacturing industries were 20 percent less than in manufacturing industries.

The specific mix of industries in a state will determine how much globalization and the shift to services affect it. States that have relied on manufacturing, such as midwestern states with auto factories or southern states with textile plants, have been hard hit, for example. Similarly, the effects of technological change, discussed below, will differ based on the make-up of a state's economy.

Technology also plays a role in wage inequality, though its magnitude is often exaggerated. Previously, a number of researchers, observing that wages for highly educated workers have risen even as the number of these workers has grown, concluded that technological change has increased the demand for educated workers and thus is a major factor in the growing pay gap between high- and lower-wage workers. But there is little evidence that this dynamic intensified much over the period in which wage inequality was growing most quickly. Thus, technology must have played a smaller role in the *increase* in wage inequality than is often claimed.

More recent research has found a different, more nuanced relationship between technology and inequality. One influential recent study argues that technological change has had little effect on the wage gap between high-wage and low-wage workers in recent years. The authors argue that since the 1980s, demand for higher-skilled, better-educated workers has driven wage increases at the *high* end of the wage scale, but wages also grew at the low end of the scale because of the continued demand for workers performing non-routine manual jobs that computers cannot perform. In the middle, however, routine jobs performed by moderately educated workers were more likely to be replaced by technology or outsourced, so these workers' wages fell.

The Decline in Union Membership

The continued decline in the percentage of workers who are union members has also contributed to increased wage inequality. Between 1979 and 2011, the percentage of workers belonging to unions dropped from 23.4 percent to 11.8 percent. By 2011, only 6.9 percent of private-sector workers were union members, compared to 37 percent of public-sector employees.

There is a point at which families can no longer increase their work effort to offset declining wages, and the United States may be approaching that limit.

Unions have historically succeeded in both raising wages and benefits and in lowering wage inequality by standardizing compensation across competing employers. Non-unionized workers typically are paid lower wages, have less job security, receive fewer benefits, and are more likely to work part time than union members. Economic analysis of the decline in union participation during the 1980s confirms that declining unionization contributes to increased earnings inequality.

One factor that has accelerated the decline of unions is the proliferation of state laws that prohibit unions from requiring union membership for all workers covered by a union contract. These so-called "right-to-work" laws are common in the South.

The Impact of Demographic Changes

Demographic changes may also contribute to the growing wage gap. For example, the share of households composed of single individuals rose from 22 percent to 27 percent between 1979 and 2010, while the share of families headed by a woman rose from 14.3 percent to 19.6 percent. These trends have reduced incomes at the low end of the income scale because both single-individual families and female-headed families generally have lower incomes. This report adjusts the income of households for the number of members so the changes in inequality reflected here do *not* result from the increase in families composed of single individuals, but to some degree they do reflect the increase in families headed by a single woman.

Another significant demographic trend, the increase in husband-wife families in which the wife works outside the home, has *lessened* income inequality among families. During the 1970s and 1980s, increasing numbers of women entered the workforce, in part to help stem the decline in family incomes that resulted from the fall in average male earnings. In addition, family members increased their hours of work. However, there is a point at which families can no longer increase their work effort to offset declining wages, and the United States may be approaching that limit. In the 1990s, wives' hours of work grew much more slowly than in the 1980s. Between 2000 and 2009, wives' hours of work declined as a result of the weak labor market.

Some have identified immigration as a potential cause of rising wage inequality. In theory, inequality would increase if the growth in the number of immigrants increases the supply of low-wage workers, thereby lowering wages at the bottom of the wage scale. The actual role of immigration in wage inequality is much less clear, however. A 2005 report from the Congressional Budget Office reviewed the research in this area and concluded, "The arrival of large numbers of immigrants with little education probably slows the growth of the wages of native-born high school dropouts, at least initially, but the ultimate impact on wages is difficult to quantify." A recent study by economists at the Federal Reserve Bank of Atlanta found only a very small negative impact (0.15 percent) on the wages of documented workers in firms that also hire undocumented workers. They also found that immigration increased wages slightly in sectors where there are opportunities for task specialization and in industries where communication skills are important.

Outside of its effect on wages, if any, immigration has been shown to reduce inequality. For example, a study in a state with many immigrants, New York, found that immigrants have expanded the number of families in the middle of the income distribution thus reducing inequality.

The potential impact of immigration on wage inequality—whether positive or negative—in a given state will depend in part on the number of immigrants in the state. For example, fewer than 5 percent of Montana and Wyoming residents are foreign-born, compared to over 20 percent of California and New York residents. Where immigrants make up a smaller share of the workforce, they will have less potential influence on wage levels.

The Impact of Government Policies

Increasing wage inequality results initially from changes in the wages that employers pay. Government policies, however, also affect income inequality, both directly (by redistributing income through the tax system and through transfer programs such as unemployment insurance and food stamps) and indirectly (through the rules and regulations that apply to private markets, such as minimum wages, tariffs, and the rules governing the formation of unions).

> *Investment income primarily accrues to those at the top of the income scale, so any increase in investment income as a share of total personal income . . . will widen income inequality.*

Labor-market policies have had a major impact on wage inequality. The real value of the federal minimum wage has declined considerably since its high point in the late 1960s. By

2011, its value was still 13 percent less than in 1979, despite four legislated increases during the 1990s and three more in the 2000s. The minimum wage is not indexed to inflation—that is, it does not increase automatically as the cost of living increases—so its real value will continue to erode each year unless Congress acts. The impact of this reduction in the minimum wage since 1979 on wage inequality has been, by many accounts, very substantial, especially for low-wage women workers.

Many states now have their own, higher minimum wage, which reduces inequality by raising wages at the bottom of the wage scale. . . .

States also play a major role in delivering safety net assistance, which pushes back against growing inequality by helping low-wage workers move up the income ladder and by shielding the most vulnerable citizens from the long-term effects of poverty.

The Shift from Labor Income to Capital Income

Besides wages, the other major source of income is capital income: Investments that yield dividends, rent, interest, and capital gains. Investment income primarily accrues to those at the top of the income scale, so any increase in investment income as a share of total personal income—as occurred over the last three decades—will widen income inequality.

Between 1979 and 2007, capital income rose as a share of personal market-based income from 15 percent to 20 percent, while labor income (wages, salaries, and fringe benefits) fell from 76 percent of personal income to 71 percent. Further, the share of national income growth going to corporate profits during the recovery from the recent recession was considerably higher than average.

One result of these trends is that the gains of economic growth show up increasingly as capital income such as interest and dividends rather than increased wages, salaries, or benefits. Thus, wage earners benefit less from economic growth than wealthier owners of assets like stocks and investment properties. A recent Economic Policy Institute analysis of the reasons why wage growth has lagged behind growth in the economy (measured by productivity growth) found that almost half of the increase in this gap since 2000 can be explained by the shift in shares of income from labor to capital.

Higher-income families benefit disproportionately from the increase in the importance of investment income, since it makes up a larger share of their total income. In 2012, 87 percent of all capital gains income will go to families in the top 5 percent of the income distribution.

Income Inequality Has Eroded the Middle Class and the American Dream

Stewart Lansley

Stewart Lansley is a visiting fellow at the Townsend Centre for International Poverty Research and the author of The Cost of Inequality: Why Economic Equality Is Essential for Recovery.

Inequality is now one of the biggest political and economic challenges facing the United States. Not that long ago, the gap between rich and poor barely registered on the political Richter scale. Now the growing income divide, an issue that dominated the [2012] presidential election debate, has turned into one of the hottest topics of the age.

From Diamond to Hourglass

Postwar American history divides into two halves. For the first three decades, those on middle and low incomes did well out of rising prosperity and inequality fell. In the second half, roughly from the mid-1970s, this process went into reverse. Set on apparent autopilot, the gains from growth were heavily colonized by the superrich, leaving the bulk of the workforce with little better than stagnant incomes.

The return of inequality to levels last seen in the 1920s has had a profound effect on American society, its values, and its economy. The United States led the world in the building of a majority middle class. As early as 1956, the celebrated sociologist, C. Wright Mills, wrote that American society had become "less a pyramid with a flat base than a fat diamond with a bulging middle."

Stewart Lansley, "The Hourglass Society," *Los Angeles Review of Books*, May 28, 2013. This article was originally published in the *Los Angeles Review of Books* (www.lareviewof books.org). Reproduced by permission.

That bulge has been on a diet. The chairman of President [Barack] Obama's Council of Economic Advisers—Professor Alan Krueger—has shown how the size of the American middle class (households with annual incomes within 50 percent of the midpoint of the income distribution) has been heading backwards from a peak of more than a half in the late 1970s to 40 percent now. The "diamond" has gone. The social shape of America now looks more like a contorted "hourglass" with a pronounced bulge at the top, a long thin stem in the middle, and a fat bulge at the bottom.

The Growing Worry About Inequality

One of the most significant effects of America's hourglass society has been the capping of opportunities and the emergence of downward mobility amongst the middle classes, a process that began well before the recession. Around 100 million Americans—a third of the population—live below or fractionally above the poverty level. A quarter of the American workforce end up in low-paid jobs, the highest rate across rich nations, while the wealthiest 400 Americans have the same combined wealth as the poorest half—over 150 million people.

It is now being increasingly argued that the levels of income concentration in recent times have had a significant negative effect on the economy.

With a growing percentage of the current generation facing a lower living standard than their parents, more and more US citizens express a "fear of falling," worried about a further loss of livelihood and their relative income status. The nation is at last waking up to what has been reality for years—the vaunted American Dream (the ability of citizens to go from rags to riches, and one of the country's most enduring values) is increasingly a myth.

In a poll conducted for *The Washington Post* before the 2012 presidential election, respondents were asked which was the bigger worry: "unfairness in the economic system that favors the wealthy" or "over-regulation of the free market that interferes with growth and prosperity." They chose unfairness by a margin of 52–37 percent. The mostly pro-self-reliant American public are perhaps coming to recognize that their much-heralded virtues of hard work and self-help are no longer an effective means to economic advancement.

An Influential Theory About Inequality

The most damaging impact of growing inequality has been on the American—and global—economy. It has been one of the central rules of market economics that inequality is good for growth and stability. The idea was enshrined in the postwar writings of the New Right critics of the model of managed capitalism that emerged after the war. "Inequality of wealth and incomes is the cause of the masses' well being, not the cause of anybody's distress" wrote the Austrian-American economist Ludwig von Mises, one of the leading prophets of the superiority of markets, in 1955.

It was a theory that gained traction during the global economic crisis of the 1970s and with the publication in 1975 of a highly influential book, *Equality and Efficiency: The Big Tradeoff*, by the late American mainstream economist Arthur Okun. This theory—that you can have either more equal societies or more economically successful ones, but not both—has been used to justify the growth of inequality in the United States, a trend that has since spread to a majority of the rich world. One of the telling by-products of the current economic crisis is that this theory is now being challenged. It is now being increasingly argued that the levels of income concentration in recent times have had a significant negative effect on the economy, bringing slower growth and greater turbulence and contributing to both the 2008 crash and the lack of a sustained recovery.

Perhaps the most significant convert to these ideas is President Obama. A year ago [December 6, 2011], he remarked, "When middle-class families can no longer afford to buy the goods and services that businesses are selling, it drags down the entire economy from top to bottom." Addressing delegates at the annual meeting of the World Economic Forum at Davos in January 2013, Christine Lagarde, head of the International Monetary Fund, endorsed this view, "I believe that the economics profession and the policy community have downplayed inequality for too long [. . .] [A] more equal distribution of income allows for more economic stability, more sustained economic growth."

This view goes against the grain of the economic orthodoxy of the last 30 years. As the Chicago economist Robert E. Lucas, Nobel prizewinner and one of the principal architects of the pro-market, self-regulating school that has dominated economic strategy in the Anglo-Saxon world, declared in 2003, "Of the tendencies that are harmful to sound economics, the most poisonous is to focus on questions of distribution."

Despite a succession of lofty speeches [by President Obama], the best evidence is that since 2008, growth has continued to be very unevenly shared.

The Importance of the Distribution Question

A growing body of evidence and opinion now holds that this idea is wrong. In fact, the "distribution question"—how the cake is divided, between wages and profits on the one hand, and between the top and bottom on the other—is critical to economic health. Over the last 30 years, the rich world, led by the United States, has steered a growing share of national output first to profits and ultimately to the top one percent. Across the 34 richest nations in the world, the share going to wages has fallen from over 66 percent in 1990 to less than 62 percent today. The result is a growing detachment of living standards from output. The stagnating incomes of the bulk of Americans, along with the shrinking of the middle, are the mirror image of the rise of the plutocracy and the return of the gilded age.

This decoupling of wages from output creates a critical structural fault that ultimately brings self-destruction. First, a growing pay output gap sucks consumer lifeblood out of economies. To fill this growing demand gap, levels of personal debt were allowed to explode. In the US, the level of outstanding personal debt rose almost threefold in the decade from 1997 to $14.4 trillion. This helped to fuel a domestic boom from the mid-1990s, but one that was never going to be sustainable.

Secondly, the long wage squeeze and the growing concentration of income at the top led to record corporate surpluses and an explosion of personal fortunes. Instead of being used to create new wealth via an investment and entrepreneurial boom (as predicted by market theorists), these massive cash surpluses were used to finance a wave of speculative financial activity and asset restructuring. The effect was the upward redistribution of existing wealth and the fueling of the bubbles—in property and business—that eventually brought the global economy to its knees. That inequality is also acting as a profound drag on the prospects of recovery.

A Program for Change

A central feature of the President's annual State of the Union address on February 11 [2013] was its call to "grow the economy from the middle out," to "reignite the true engine of America's economic growth—a rising, thriving middle class." In his call for more active government to reduce inequality— from a 25 percent hike in the minimum wage to higher taxes on the rich—Obama was adding some meat to his earlier call "to restore an economy where everyone gets a fair shot, and everyone does their fair share." Yet, despite a succession of lofty speeches, the best evidence is that since 2008, growth has continued to be very unevenly shared. The economists Emmanuel Saez and Thomas Piketty have shown that over nine tenths of growth in 2010 was captured by the top one percent. This is in stark contrast to the 1930s, when the big gainers from recovery were most ordinary Americans and the big losers were the superrich.

Obama's program for change fails to match the radicalism of Franklin D. Roosevelt in the 1930s or that of Lyndon Johnson's War on Poverty three decades later. Of course, creating a more equal America is hardly a cakewalk. The United States has rarely been more divided on the politics of change. Before Congressman Paul Ryan became Mitt Romney's controversial running mate, he had blasted Obama's proposed (and modest) tax measures on the rich as "class warfare." Other global leaders seem equally disempowered in the face of the might of a global billionaire class determined to preserve its privileges, muscle, and wealth.

But unless Obama can find a way of breaking the firewalls created by the new plutocrats to protect their wealth from economic collapse and political interference, the likelihood is that the American middle class will go on shrinking, the American dream will further erode, and the nation's economy will continue to stumble from crisis to crisis.

Income Inequality Affects Social Equality, Social Unity, and Happiness

Timothy Noah

Timothy Noah is a journalist and the author of The Great Divergence: America's Growing Inequality Crisis and What We Can Do About It.

The Declaration of Independence says that all men are created equal, but we know that isn't true. George Clooney was created better-looking than me. Stephen Hawking was born smarter, Evander Holyfield stronger, Jon Stewart funnier, and Warren Buffett better able to understand financial markets. All these people have parlayed their exceptional gifts into very high incomes—much higher than mine. Is that so odd? Odder would be if Buffett or Clooney were forced to live on my income, adequate though it might be to a *petit-bourgeois* [lower middle-class] journalist. Lest you conclude my equanimity is in any way unique (we *Slate* writers are known for our contrarianism), Barbara Ehrenreich, in her 2001 book *Nickel and Dimed*, quotes a woman named Colleen, a single mother of two, saying much the same thing about the wealthy families whose floors she scrubs on hands and knees. "I don't mind, really," she says, "because I guess I'm a simple person, and I don't want what they have. I mean, it's nothing to me."

It is easy to make too much of this, and a few conservatives have done so in seeking to dismiss the importance (or even existence) of the Great Divergence. Let's look at their arguments.

The Defense of Inequality

Inequality is good. Every year the American Economic Association [AEA] invites a distinguished economist to deliver at its annual conference the Richard T. Ely Lecture. Ely, a founder of the AEA and a leader in the Progressive movement, would have been horrified by the 1999 lecture that Finis Welch, a professor of economics (now emeritus) at Texas A&M, delivered in his name. Its title was "In Defense of Inequality."

Welch began by stating that "all of economics results from inequality. Without inequality of priorities and capabilities, there would be no trade, no specialization, and no surpluses produced by cooperation." He invited his audience to consider a world in which skill, effort, and sheer chance played no role whatsoever in what you got paid. The only decision that would affect your wage level would be when to leave school. "After that, the clock ticks, and wages follow the experience path. Nothing else matters. Can you imagine a more horrible, a more deadening existence?"

> *The Great Divergence had a more significant impact on the working middle class than on the destitute.*

But something close to the dystopia Welch envisioned already exists for those toiling in the economy's lower tiers. Welch should have a chat with his office receptionist. Or he could read *Nickel and Dimed*, or the 2010 book *Catching Out* by Dick J. Reavis, a contributing editor at *Texas Monthly* who went undercover as a day laborer. Waitresses, construction workers, dental assistants, call-center operators—people in these jobs are essentially replaceable, and usually have bosses who don't distinguish between individual initiative and insubordination. Even experience is of limited value, because it's often accompanied by diminishing physical vigor.

Welch said that he believed inequality was destructive only when "the low-wage citizenry views society as unfair, when it views effort as not worthwhile, when upward mobility is impossible or so unlikely that its pursuit is not worthwhile." Colleen's comment would appear to suggest that the first of these conditions has not been met. But that's only because I omitted what she went on to say: "But what I would like is to be able to take a day off now and then ... if I had to ... and still be able to buy groceries the next day." Colleen may not begrudge the rich the material goods they've acquired through skill, effort, and sheer chance, but that doesn't mean she thinks her own labors secure her an adequate level of economic security. Clearly, they don't.

The thought that the have-nots are compensating for their lower incomes by putting themselves (and the country) in economically ruinous hock is not reassuring.

Welch judged the growing financial rewards accruing to those with higher levels of education a good thing insofar as they provided an incentive to go to college or graduate school. But for most of the 20th century, smaller financial incentives attracted enough workers to meet the economy's growing demand for higher-skilled labor. That demand isn't being met today, as Harvard economists Claudia Goldin and Lawrence Katz have shown. Welch also said that both women and blacks made income gains during the Great Divergence. But that's hardly evidence that growing income inequality unrelated to gender or race doesn't matter. Finally, Welch argued that the welfare state has made it too easy not to work at all. But the Great Divergence had a more significant impact on the working middle class than on the destitute.

The Relevance of Income

Income doesn't matter. In most contexts, libertarians can fairly be said to place income in very high regard. Tax it to even the slightest degree and they cry foul. If government assistance must be extended, they prefer a cash transaction to the provision of government services. The market is king, and what is the market if not a mighty river of money?

Bring up the topic of growing income inequality, though, and you're likely to hear a different tune. Case in point: "Thinking Clearly About Economic Inequality," a 2009 Cato Institute paper by Will Wilkinson. Income isn't what matters, Wilkinson argues; consumption is, and "the weight of the evidence shows that the run-up in consumption inequality has been considerably less dramatic than the rise in income inequality." Wilkinson concedes that the available data on consumption are shakier than the available data on income; he might also have mentioned that consumption in excess of income usually means debt—as in, say, subprime mortgages. The thought that the have-nots are compensating for their lower incomes by putting themselves (and the country) in economically ruinous hock is not reassuring.

Wilkinson further argues that consumption isn't what matters; what matters is utility gained from consumption. Joe and Sam both own refrigerators. Joe's is a $350 model from Ikea. Sam's is an $11,000 state-of-the-art Sub-Zero. Sam gets to consume a lot more than Joe, but whatever added utility he achieves is marginal; Joe's Ikea fridge "will keep your beer just as cold." But if getting rich is only a matter of spending more money on the same stuff you'd buy if you were poor, why bother to climb the greasy pole at all?

The Relevance of Buying Power

Next Wilkinson decides that utility isn't what matters; what matters is buying power. Food is cheaper than ever before. Since lower-income people spend their money disproportionately on food, declining food prices, Wilkinson argues, constitute a sort of raise. Never mind that Ehrenreich routinely found, in her travels among the lower middle class, workers who routinely skipped lunch to save money or brought an individual-size pack of junk food and called that lunch. Reavis reports that a day laborer's typical lunch budget is $3. That won't buy much. The problem isn't the cost of food per se but the cost of shelter, which has shot up so high that low-income families don't have much left over to spend on other essentials.

Declining food prices constitute a sort of raise for higher-income people too. But Wilkinson writes that the affluent spend a smaller share of their budget on food and a much larger share on psychotherapy and yoga and cleaning services. And since services like these are unaffected by foreign competition or new efficiencies in manufacturing, Wilkinson argues, providers can charge whatever they like.

Tell it to Colleen! I recently worked out with my new cleaning lady what I would pay her. Here's how the negotiation went. I told her what I would pay her. She said, "OK." According to the Bureau of Labor Statistics, the median income for a housekeeper is $19,250, which is $2,800 below the poverty line for a family of four.

Among industrialized nations, those that have achieved the greatest social equality are the same ones that have achieved the greatest income equality.

The Impact of Social Equality

A more thoughtful version of the income-doesn't-matter argument surfaces in my former *Slate* colleague Mickey Kaus' 1992 book *The End of Equality*. Kaus chided "Money Liberals" for trying to redistribute income when instead they might be working to diminish social inequality by creating or shoring up spheres in which rich and poor are treated the same. Everybody can picnic in the park. Everybody should be able to receive decent health care. Under a compulsory national service program, everybody would be required to perform some civilian or military duty.

As a theoretical proposition, Kaus' vision is appealing. Bill Gates will always have lots more money than me, no matter how progressive the tax system becomes. But if he gets called to jury duty he has to show up, just like me. When his driver's license expires, he'll be just as likely to have to take a driving test. Why not expand this egalitarian zone to, say, education, by making public schools so good that Gates' grandchildren will be as likely to attend them as mine or yours?

But at a practical level, Kaus' exclusive reliance on social equality is simply inadequate. For one thing, the existing zones of social equality are pretty circumscribed. Neither Gates nor I spend a lot of time hanging around the Department of Motor Vehicles. Rebuilding or creating the more meaningful spheres—say, public education or a truly national health care system—won't occur overnight. Nurturing the social-equality sphere isn't likely to pay off for a very long time.

Kaus would like to separate social equality from income equality, but the two go hand in hand. In theory they don't have to, but in practice they just do. Among industrialized nations, those that have achieved the greatest social equality are the same ones that have achieved the greatest income equality. France, for example, has a level of income inequality much lower than that of most other countries in the Organization for Economic Cooperation and Development. It's one of the very few places where income inequality has been going down. (Most everywhere else it's gone up, though nowhere to the degree it has in the United States.) France also enjoys what the World Health Organization [WHO] calls the world's finest health care system (by which the WHO means, in large part, the most egalitarian one; this is the famous survey from 2000 in which the U.S. ranked 37th).

Do France's high marks on both social equality and income equality really strike you as a coincidence? As incomes become more unequal, a likelier impulse among the rich isn't to urge or even allow the government to create or expand public institutions where they can mix it up with the proles [working class]. It's to create or expand private institutions that will help them maintain separation from the proles with whom they have less and less in common. According to Jonathan Rowe, who has written extensively about social equality, that's exactly what's happening in the United States. In an essay titled "The Vanishing Commons" that appeared in *Inequality Matters*, a 2005 anthology, Rowe notes that Congress has been busy extending copyright terms and patent monopolies and turning over public lands to mining and timber companies for below-market fees. "In an 'ownership' society especially," Rowe writes, "we should think about what we own in common, not just what we keep apart."

Inequality and Happiness

Inequality doesn't create unhappiness. Arthur C. Brooks, president of the American Enterprise Institute, argued this point in *National Review* online in June. What drives entrepreneurs, he wrote, is not the desire for money but the desire for earned success. When people feel they deserve their success, they are happy; when they do not, they aren't. "The money is just the metric of the value that the person is creating."

People do not experience life as an interesting moment in the evolution of human societies. They experience it in the present and weigh their own experience against that of the living.

Brooks marshaled very little evidence to support his argument, and what evidence he did muster was less impressive than he thought. He made much of a 1996 survey that asked people how successful they felt, and how happy. Among the 45 percent who counted themselves "completely successful" or "very successful," 39 percent said they were very happy. Among the 55 percent who counted themselves at most "somewhat successful," only 20 percent said they were happy. Brooks claimed victory with the finding that successful people were more likely to be happy (or at least to say they were), by 19 percentage points, than less-successful people. More striking, though, was that 61 percent of the successful people—a significant majority—did not say they were "very happy." Nowhere in the survey were the successful people asked whether they deserved their happiness.

Let's grant Brooks his generalization that people who believe they deserve their success are likelier to be happy than people who believe they don't. It makes intuitive sense. But Brooks' claim that money is only a "metric" does not. Looking at the same survey data, Berkeley sociologist Michael Hout found that from 1973 to 2000 the difference between the affluent and the poor who counted themselves either "very happy" or "not too happy" ranged from 19 percentage points to 27. Among the poor, the percentage who felt "very happy" fell by nearly one-third from 1973 to 1994, then crept up a couple of points during the tight labor market of the late 1990s. Hout also observed that overall happiness dropped a modest 5 percent from 1973 to 2000.

Quality of life is improving. This argument has been made by too many conservatives to count. Yes, it's true that an unemployed steelworker living in the 21st century is in many important ways better off than the royals and aristocrats of yesteryear. Living conditions improve over time. But people do not experience life as an interesting moment in the evolution of human societies. They experience it in the present and weigh their own experience against that of the living. Brooks cites (even though it contradicts his argument) a famous 1998 study by economists Sara Solnick (then at the University of

Miami, now at the University of Vermont) and David Hemenway of the Harvard School of Public Health. Subjects were asked which they'd prefer: to earn $50,000 while knowing everyone else earned $25,000, or to earn $100,000 while knowing everyone else earned $200,000. Objectively speaking, $100,000 is twice as much as $50,000. Even so, 56 percent chose $50,000 if it meant that would put them on top rather than at the bottom. We are social creatures and establish our expectations relative to others.

The Denial of Increasing Inequality

Inequality isn't increasing. This is the boldest line of conservative attack, challenging a consensus about income trends in the United States that most conservatives accept. (Brooks: "It is factually incorrect to argue that income inequality has not risen in America—it has.") Alan Reynolds, a senior fellow at Cato, made the case in a January 2007 paper. It was a technical argument hinging largely on a critique of the tax data used by Emmanuel Saez and Thomas Piketty in the groundbreaking paper we looked at in our installment about the superrich. But as Gary Burtless of Brookings noted in a January 2007 reply, Social Security records "tell a simple and similar story." A Congressional Budget Office analysis, Burtless wrote, addressed "almost all" of Reynolds' objections to Saez and Piketty's findings, and confirmed "a sizable rise in both pre-tax and after-tax inequality." Reynolds' paper didn't deny notable increases in top incomes, but he argued that these were because of technical changes in tax law and/or to isolated and unusual financial events. That, Burtless answered, was akin to arguing that, "adjusting for the weather and the season, no homeowner in New Orleans ended up with a wet basement" after Hurricane Katrina.

That income inequality very much matters is the thesis of the 2009 book *The Spirit Level*, by Richard Wilkinson and Kate Pickett, two medical researchers based in Yorkshire. The book has been criticized for overreaching. Wilkinson and Pickett relate income inequality trends not only to mental and physical health, violence, and teenage pregnancy, but also to global warming. But their larger point—that income inequality is bad not only for people on the losing end but also for society at large—seems hard to dispute. "Modern societies," they write,

> will depend increasingly on being creative, adaptable, inventive, well-informed and flexible communities, able to respond generously to each other and to needs wherever they arise. These are characteristics not of societies in hock to the rich, in which people are driven by status insecurities, but of populations used to working together and respecting each other as equals.

There is a reason why, in years past, Americans scorned societies starkly divided into the privileged and the destitute.

The United States' economy is currently struggling to emerge from a severe recession brought on by the financial crisis of 2008. Was that crisis brought about by income inequality? Some economists are starting to think it may have been. David Moss of Harvard Business School has produced an intriguing chart that shows bank failures tend to coincide with periods of growing income inequality. "I could hardly believe how tight the fit was," he told the *New York Times*. Princeton's [economist] Paul Krugman has similarly been considering whether the Great Divergence helped cause the recession by pushing middle-income Americans into debt. The growth of household debt has followed a pattern strikingly similar to the growth in income inequality. Raghuram G. Rajan, a business school professor at the University of Chicago, recently argued on the *New Republic*'s Web site that "let them eat credit" was "the mantra of the political establishment in the go-go years before the crisis." Christopher Brown, an economist at Arkansas State University, wrote a paper in 2004 affirming that "inequality can exert a significant drag on effective demand." Reducing inequality, he argued, would also reduce consumer debt. Today, Brown's paper looks prescient.

The Growing Income Chasm

Heightened partisanship in Washington and declining trust in government have many causes (and the latter slide predates the Great Divergence). But surely the growing income chasm between the poor and middle class and the rich, between the Sort of Rich and the Rich, and even between the Rich and the Stinking Rich, make it especially difficult to reestablish any spirit of *e pluribus unum* [out of many, one]. Republicans and Democrats compete to show which party more fervently opposes the elite, with each side battling to define what "elite" means. In a more equal society, the elite would still be resented. But I doubt that opposing it would be an organizing principle of politics to the same extent that it is today.

I find myself returning to the gut-level feeling expressed at the start of this series: I do not wish to live in a banana republic [a country operated as a commercial enterprise for private profit]. There is a reason why, in years past, Americans scorned societies starkly divided into the privileged and the destitute. They were repellent. Is it my imagination, or do we hear less criticism of such societies today in the United States? Might it be harder for Americans to sustain in such discussions the necessary sense of moral superiority?

What is the ideal distribution of income in society? I couldn't tell you, and historically much mischief has been accomplished by addressing this question too precisely. But I can tell you this: We've been headed in the wrong direction for far too long.

There Is No Evidence That Inequality Harms the Economy or Democracy

Scott Winship

Scott Winship is a fellow in economic studies at the Brookings Institution.

In recent years, inequality has become the core economic concern of the American left. The gap between the haves and have-nots is understood to be the fatal flaw of our economic system—a fundamental problem that is the source of countless other difficulties. To hear many liberals tell it, increasing inequality is holding back growth, crushing the prospects of the poor and middle class, and even undermining American democracy. Such concerns are prominent in President [Barack] Obama's rhetoric, and seem also to drive key parts of his policy agenda—especially the relentless pursuit of higher taxes on the wealthy. As the president put it in his second inaugural address in January [2013], he believes "that our country cannot succeed when a shrinking few do very well and a growing many barely make it."

The Arguments About Inequality

The idea that our economy is held back by inequality is echoed in the claims of some of the nation's most prominent economists. Princeton professor (and Nobel laureate) Paul Krugman and David Card of the University of California, Berkeley, contend that inequality hurts economic mobility. Princeton's Alan Krueger (now chairman of the White House Council of Economic Advisers) and Columbia's Joseph Stiglitz (another Nobelist) think it dampens economic growth. Along with Raghuram Rajan, former chief economist of the International Monetary Fund [IMF], Stiglitz also argues that inequality was behind the financial crisis. Cornell economist Robert Frank and former labor secretary Robert Reich are convinced that it fuels the indebtedness of the middle class. The Massachusetts Institute of Technology's Daron Acemoglu believes that inequality enables economic elites to capture the machinery of government and thus ultimately produces national decline.

But while the credentials of these advocates may be impressive, their arguments are not. Some of these economists seem to think that arguments made for popular audiences do not require the same rigor demanded in academic papers. Others won their well-earned accolades doing groundbreaking research on subjects unrelated to the consequences of inequality and have little expertise in this area. In some cases, these authors examine inequality in America in light of findings from developing countries, failing to acknowledge that the circumstances of those other nations are so different from ours that they render this research inapplicable to the United States. In still other cases, these economists carelessly mistake correlation for causation.

Taken together, their errors severely undermine the liberal case about the consequences of inequality. True, a careful examination of the evidence does not establish that inequality is harmless, or that it has nothing to do with our other economic problems. Economic data cannot prove a negative. But they can fail to prove a positive, and they do fail to prove the claims that underlie the left's basic economic narrative. They reveal little basis for thinking that inequality is at the root of our economic challenges, and therefore for believing that reducing inequality would meaningfully address our lagging growth, enable greater mobility, avert future financial crises, or secure America's democratic institutions.

The Relationship Between Growth and Inequality

Perhaps the most common assertion regarding the ill effects of inequality in our time is that an unequal economy just doesn't work for most people—that inequality impedes growth and harms standards of living. Stiglitz recently declared that, "with inequality at its highest level since before the Depression, a robust recovery will be difficult in the short term, and the American dream—a good life in exchange for hard work—is slowly dying." Less dramatically, Krueger's much-publicized inequality speech at the Center for American Progress in early 2012 included the claim that "the economy would be in better shape and aggregate demand would be stronger if the size of the middle class had not dwindled as a result of rising inequality."

The problem is not simply that evidence of inequality's alleged harm to growth is inconclusive or imprecise. There is also significant evidence to the contrary, which throws the left's conclusions about inequality into doubt.

There are a number of reasons why, in theory, inequality might reduce growth. It might dampen overall consumption: The rich spend proportionally less of their incomes than the non-rich do, and when a greater portion of the nation's overall wealth flows to those who will not use it for direct consumption, economic activity could decline. Inequality might reduce entrepreneurship by saddling college graduates from lower-income families with crushing student debt. It might stifle growth by reducing workers' motivation, happiness, and social trust, which would tend to reduce their productivity. Or it might cause talent to be allocated less efficiently by closing off paths to success for people who do not start out rich.

Inequality has been accused of having all of these effects. But does it in fact reduce growth? There is no clear evidence that it does. In a long paper purporting to show how inequality reduces economic growth, Heather Boushey and Adam Hersh of the Center for American Progress concede early on that the literature that directly examines this question is inconclusive and largely inapplicable to America's circumstances:

> There is, of course, a rich literature on the relationship between inequality and growth.... Although there are many conflicting views, there is ample evidence that inequality can, in fact, hurt growth under many circumstances. But this literature focuses mostly on the experience of developing countries, and its applicability to the challenges currently facing the United States is not entirely clear.

Indeed, one of the most widely cited papers in the inequality debates—a 2011 study by IMF economists Andrew Berg and Jonathan Ostry showing that inequality hurts growth—suffers from this very problem of focusing primarily on developing countries. Even putting aside the applicability of these studies, Boushey and Hersh conclude from their review that, "Ultimately, data and methodological issues mean that analyses are too imprecise to deliver definitive answers to this old and central question in economics research."

But the problem is not simply that evidence of inequality's alleged harm to growth is inconclusive or imprecise. There is also significant evidence to the contrary, which throws the left's conclusions about inequality into doubt. Recent work by Harvard's Christopher Jencks (with Dan Andrews and Andrew Leigh) shows that, over the course of the 20th century, within the United States and across developed countries, there was no relationship between changes in inequality and economic growth. In fact, between 1960 and 2000, rising inequality coincided with *higher* growth across these countries. In forthcoming work, University of Arizona sociologist Lane Kenworthy also finds that, since 1979, higher growth in the share of income held by the top 1% of earners has been associated with stronger economic growth across several countries.

Inequality and Wage Growth

If there is scant evidence of a link between inequality and poor economic growth, what of the link between growing inequality and stagnating wages? The belief that such a connection exists is, after all, at the core of the left's nostalgia for the golden age that followed World War II, when the economy boomed and distributed its benefits broadly across the American population. *New Republic* senior editor Timothy Noah spoke for many on the left when he wrote in his recent book *The Great Divergence* that "there probably was no better time to hold membership in America's middle class" than the 1950s and '60s.

> *If inequality between the poor and middle class is problematic, it has always been problematic—even during the left's supposed golden age—and is not especially so today.*

This widely held view is a function of muddling the difference between people's well-being and the rate at which that well-being improves. The fact is that the median family today has nearly twice the purchasing power of its counterpart in 1960. The basic well-being of today's family is significantly better than that of a family living in the supposed golden age. The issue is that this modern family's income is growing more slowly than that of its 1960 counterpart, while the incomes of Americans at the top of the income scale are growing far faster. For Noah and others, it could not be more obvious that the latter development accounts for the former—that inequality is holding back middle-class income growth. In this view, even if the middle class is not actually worse off than it used to be, it is being hurt by the growing fortunes of society's richest.

But this claim, too, is vastly oversimplified and lacking a solid empirical foundation. The nature of inequality's rise over recent decades has been poorly understood even by many economists. . . .

The Link Between Prosperity and Inequality

Between 1969 and 2007, incomes for Americans in the bottom fifth of the income distribution rose by 46%, compared with a 63% increase for Americans in the middle fifth. Put another way, if inequality between the poor and middle class is problematic, it has always been problematic—even during the left's supposed golden age—and is not especially so today.

The story is quite different when comparing the poor or the middle class to the richest Americans—so-called "high-end inequality." This type of inequality has risen steadily and dramatically since 1979, after declining over the prior 30 years. In the 1950s, '60s, and '70s, the poor and middle class saw bigger gains than the rich. Since 1979, the incomes of the top 5% of earners have risen more than four times as much as the incomes of the bottom fifth and more than three times as much as those of the middle fifth. The increase for the top 1% has been even more dramatic, and the disparities only grow as one moves higher and higher up the income distribution.

But is it likely that this dramatically increased prosperity for the wealthiest Americans has suppressed income growth for everyone else? Some of the gains made by those at the top could not have accrued to people lower on the income ladder in any event: For instance, had Chinese investors not enriched bankers in New York, their money would surely have gone to bankers in London or Frankfurt—not to workers in middle America. Moreover, by promoting economic efficiency and broad growth, at least *some* gains at the top actually make non-rich families better off. And the experience of the recent recession suggests that people lower on the income distribution do not benefit when the wealthiest Americans earn less: Between 2007 and 2009, when the share of total U.S. pre-tax income received by the top 1% of earners fell from 18.7% to 13.4% (erasing the gains of the previous five years), median income fell by 5%. Cato Institute scholar Alan Reynolds notes that the poverty rate tends to fall when the share of income received by the top 1% rises (and vice versa). Looking across several developed nations (including the United States), Lane Kenworthy finds that increases in inequality may lower median incomes somewhat. But when he allows for the possibility that inequality might increase economic growth rates and lead to greater government redistribution, the effect disappears.

When it comes to recent inequality trends, appearances can be deceiving.

The Issue of Wage Stagnation

As to the claim that the incomes of most Americans have stagnated during the period in which those of the wealthiest Americans have soared, Burkhauser's figures suggest otherwise. His research shows that the middle fifth of the income distribution was actually more than one-third richer in 2007 than it was in 1979. The Congressional Budget Office corroborates this estimate, and research by the University of Chicago's Bruce Meyer and Notre Dame's James Sullivan suggests that the increase may have been 50% or more. Such growth could be called "stagnation" only in relation to the golden age of the post-war boom, when the incomes of the middle fifth of Americans doubled over 20 years. Income growth has certainly slowed for poor and middle-class families since then, and not only in the United States: In a range of European and English-speaking countries, demographics and other factors have combined to yield lower rates of economic growth. But there is simply no clear evidence that this slower growth is being caused by rising inequality.

It may be true that the government could redistribute at least some income between rich and poor Americans such that the benefits to the poor exceeded the harm done to the rich. But justifying such redistribution requires making a persuasive and empirically grounded case that the status quo is unfair. Analysts such as Jared Bernstein (of the Center on Budget and Policy Priorities) often claim that worker pay has not kept up with productivity, citing this as evidence that gains at the top were effectively stolen from the middle. While it is true that wage increases have lagged behind productivity growth in recent decades, my ongoing research suggests a simple explanation: Compensation outpaced productivity growth during the mid-20th century (in the peak years of unionism), and recent decades have seen a correction in which productivity levels have had to catch up to pay. On balance, the numbers still favor workers: If President William McKinley had been told in 1900 how much higher productivity would be in 2013 and had used that information to guess how much higher hourly compensation would be, his prediction would have been too *low*.

Of course, one can argue that workers' pay increases should outpace growth in the value of what they produce, which is apparently what happened when a greater share of the work force was unionized. But one cannot use productivity trends as evidence that the rich have unfairly siphoned off what rightfully belongs to workers. In other words, when it comes to recent inequality trends, appearances can be deceiving. What has looked like gains for the wealthy coming at the expense of the poor and middle class turns out to be, in historical context, an enduring victory for workers in an 80-year tug of war with capital. The notion that inequality is stifling economic growth or suppressing the wages of the middle class is simply not supported by the available evidence. . . .

The Link Between Inequality and Democracy

The liberal tale of inequality's consequences extends beyond economics into politics. A number of prominent economists—along with a few highly visible political scientists—have worried in recent years that rising inequality might pose some threat to democracy. They have suggested that growing income divides may reduce voting or other forms of participation that require time and money, and have expressed fear that these disparities will allow the rich to buy elections or make elected officials unduly responsive to those with deep pockets.

Economists Daron Acemoglu of MIT and James Robinson of Harvard take this line of reasoning to its logical conclusion: On the basis of evidence from developing countries, they argue that inequality leads the rich and the representatives they buy to establish extractive political institutions that direct redistribution upward. And Acemoglu and Robinson believe— but make little effort to show—that this evidence has direct implications for American inequality. Political scientists Nolan McCarty, Keith Poole, and Howard Rosenthal have even argued that rising inequality has caused the political polarization now seen in our national politics. Their evidence basically amounts to the same "things got worse over the same period in which inequality rose" case used to argue that economic inequality has diminished opportunity. Again, correlation and causation are harmfully confounded.

The truth is that political science has only begun to consider these questions and has yet to reach any consensus. Many in the field are well aware of this inconclusiveness. In 2004, the American Political Science Association Task Force on Inequality and American Democracy concluded, "We know little about the connections between changing economic inequality and changes in political behavior, governing institutions, and public policy." The past eight years have not seen new research that ought to alter that conclusion.

Policy Preferences Across Income Groups

Meanwhile, in 2008, Peter Enns and Christopher Wlezien convened a conference to consider the question of whether elected officials are more responsive to the preferences of some citizens than to those of others. Their 2011 book, *Who Gets Represented?*, summarized the outcome:

> We discovered that no real consensus exists on how different groups [including those defined by income] influence policy. Not only were there debates about differences between groups, there were also serious disagreements about whether these differences matter. . . . [T]he conference made clear that we do not yet have a good answer to the question of who gets represented.

The claims of inequality's political effects are even more difficult to demonstrate, and even more poorly established empirically, than are the claims of its economic effects.

Enns and Wlezien examined how policy preferences differ between rich, middle-class, and poor Americans. They found that the three groups have very similar preferences for increasing public spending on crime, education, health, and the environment, and common preferences for spending less on defense. The poor are less supportive of reducing spending on welfare than are the middle class and rich, and they are less likely to believe their taxes are too high. But these gaps have not changed much over time and show no relationship to changes in inequality. Regarding the possibility that the preferences of the rich, middle class, and poor are unequally attended to, Enns and Wlezien conclude that "there is little difference for policymakers to represent." Other work, reported in the 2004 Russell Sage Foundation volume *Social Inequality*, finds little or no relationship across countries or in the United States over time between income inequality and government generosity to the poor. Kenworthy, too, concludes that rising inequality probably has not lowered expenditures in support of safety nets.

Recent books by political scientists Larry Bartels and Martin Gilens have received significant attention for finding that the votes of members of Congress and federal policy outcomes are more aligned with the ideological identifications and policy preferences of the rich than of the middle class or poor. In contrast, Robert Erikson and Yosef Bhatti, in a chapter in the Enns and Wlezien volume that directly addresses the Bartels research, fail to find any evidence of unequal representation. In part, they report, this is because "ideological preferences among different income strata of state electorates are almost impossible to separate statistically."

In other words, the claims of inequality's political effects are even more difficult to demonstrate, and even more poorly established empirically, than are the claims of its economic effects.

Inequality, Cause, and Effect

It is, of course, possible that future research will more rigorously and consistently identify negative effects of income inequality on economic, social, and political outcomes. The point of reviewing the existing evidence is not to argue that such effects do not exist; nor is it to argue that the things inequality is said to affect are unimportant. It is, rather, to argue that the evidence behind the liberal narrative of inequality as a driver of our social and economic woes is not nearly firm enough to support the political and policy arguments now often built upon it. One can be concerned about economic growth, financial stability, and economic mobility regardless of whether income inequality harms any of them.

Those who are convinced that inequality must have harmful consequences might interpret the case made here as simply an attempt to "muddy the waters" by raising doubt about necessarily imperfect, but nevertheless serious, research. But the motive here is quite the opposite. After all, finding statistical relationships between economic and social problems is easy; it is the failure to rigorously test hypotheses about the *meaning* of these relationships, as well as the inclination to selectively cite research friendly to one's position, that muddies the wa ters. Pointing out the limits of our knowledge is a way to clear things up.

The greater clarity made possible by such an effort should help many liberals see the need to rethink their rhetoric, if not their economic priorities. There is simply very little evidence to suggest that, within the range of inequality that modern counties have experienced and the range seen in our country over the past century, income disparities between the rich, middle class, and poor merit the intense attention lavished on them by the left.

Income Inequality Can Be Good for Everyone

Richard A. Epstein

Richard A. Epstein is the Peter and Kirsten Bedford Senior Fellow at the Hoover Institution and the Laurence A. Tisch Professor of Law at New York University Law School.

One month into the second term of the Obama administration [February 2013], the economic prognosis looks mixed at best. On growth, the U.S. Department of Commerce reports the last quarter of 2012 produced a small decline in gross domestic product, without any prospects for a quick reversal. On income inequality, the most recent statistics (which only go through 2011) focus on the top 1 percent.

"Incomes Flat in Recovery, But Not for the 1%" reports Annie Lowrey of the *New York Times*. Relying on a recent report prepared by the well-known economist Professor Emmanuel Saez, who is the director for the Center of Equitable Growth at Berkeley, Lowrey reports that the income of the top 1 percent has increased by 11.2 percent, while the overall income of the rest of the population has decreased slightly by 0.4 percent.

A Pareto Improvement

What should we make of these numbers? One approach is to stress the increase in wealth inequality, deploring the gains of the top 1 percent while lamenting the decline in the income of the remainder of the population. But this approach is only half right. We should be uneasy about any and all income declines, period. But, by the same token, we should collectively be pleased by increases in income at the top, so long as they

Richard A. Epstein, "In Praise of Income Inequality," *Defining Ideas*, February 19, 2013.

were not caused by taking, whether through taxation or regulation, from individuals at the bottom.

This conclusion rests on the notion of a Pareto improvement, which favors any changes in overall utility or wealth that make at least one person better off without making anyone else worse off. By that measure, there would be an unambiguous social improvement if the income of the wealthy went up by 100 percent so long as the income of those at the bottom end did not, as a consequence, go down. That same measure would, of course, applaud gains in the income of the 99 percent so long as the income of the top 1 percent did not fall either.

This line of thought is quite alien to thinkers like Saez, who view the excessive concentration of income as a harm even if it results from a Pareto improvement. Any center for "equitable growth" has to pay as much attention to the first constraint as it does to the second. Under Saez's view of equity, it is better to narrow the gap between the top and the bottom than to increase the overall wealth.

To see the limits of this reasoning, consider two hypothetical scenarios. In the first, 99 percent of the population has an average income of $10 and the top 1 percent has an income of $100. In the second, we increase the income gap. Now, the 99 percent earn $12 and the top 1 percent earns $130. Which scenario is better?

This hypothetical comparison captures several key points. First, *everyone* is better off with the second distribution of wealth than with the first—a clear Pareto improvement. Second, the gap between the rich and the poor in the second distribution is greater in both absolute and relative terms.

Praise for Declining Income

The stark challenge to ardent egalitarians is explaining why anyone should prefer the first distribution to the second. Many will argue for some intermediate solution. But how much wealth are they prepared to sacrifice for the sake of equality? Beyond that, they will have a hard time finding a political mechanism that could achieve a greater measure of equality and a program of equitable growth. The public choice problems, which arise from self-interested intrigue in the political arena, are hard to crack.

These unresolved tensions are revealed by looking at a passage from Saez's report *Striking it Richer*. Saez is largely indifferent to these problems of implementation when he observes ominously that

> falls in income concentration due to economic downturns are temporary unless drastic regulation and tax policy changes are implemented and prevent income concentration from bouncing back. Such policy changes took place after the Great Depression during the New Deal and permanently reduced income concentration until the 1970s. In contrast, recent downturns, such as the 2001 recession, lead to only very temporary drops in income concentration.
>
> The policy changes that are taking place coming out of the Great Recession (financial regulation and top tax rate increase in 2013) are not negligible but they are modest relative to the policy changes that took place coming out of the Great Depression. Therefore, it seems unlikely that US income concentration will fall much in the coming years.

Let's unpack this. It is surely true that the top 1 percent (or at least the top 1 percent of that 1 percent) is heavily invested in financial instruments, and thus will suffer a decline in income with the regulation of the financial markets. But by the same token, it would be absurd to praise any declines in overall capital wealth because of its supposed contribution to greater equality for all individuals. Nor would it make any sense to describe, as Saez does, the current situation as one of "booming stock-prices" when the Dow Jones Industrial Average still teeters below its 2007 high. Take into account inflation and one finds that the real capital stock of the United

States has actually declined over the last six years, which reduces the wealth available to create private sector jobs.

Nor, moreover, is there anything permanent about the 2012 gain in income at the top. As Saez himself notes, some portion of the recent income surge has resulted from a "retiming of income," by which high-income taxpayers accelerate income to 2012 to avoid the higher 2013 tax rates. Accordingly, we can expect that real incomes at the top will be lower in 2013 than otherwise would have been the case. Indeed, it is possible that these "modestly" higher taxes could produce the worst of both worlds, by depressing government revenues *and* reducing the income of the rich.

There is no sustainable way to make the poor richer by making the rich poorer.

Taxation and Regulation

Saez's own qualification is best read as a backhanded recognition of the perverse incentives that rapid changes in the tax structure create. It is a pity that he does not go one step further to accept the sound position that low, flat, and steady tax rates offer the only way—the only equitable way—to sustainable overall growth.

Unfortunately, Saez would rather move our system precisely in the opposite direction. He praises the dramatic shifts that took place during the Great Depression, when marginal tax rates at the federal level reached 62 percent under [President Herbert] Hoover's Revenue Act of 1932, and stayed high during [President Franklin] Roosevelt's New Deal period. The anemic economic performance of the Roosevelt New Deal arose in large part from a combination of high taxation and destructive national policies that strangled free trade, increased union power, and reduced overall agricultural production. Today, Saez concentrates on the income growth of the top 1 percent. He does not address the feeble levels of economic growth over the last five years.

Saez may think that the latest round of tax increases and financial regulations are "modest" in the grand scheme of things. But their effects have been predictable. The declines in productivity have translated into lower levels of income and well-being for all affected groups.

The blunt truth remains that any government-mandated leveling in society will be a leveling *down*. There is no sustainable way to make the poor richer by making the rich poorer. But increased regulation and taxation will make both groups poorer. Negative growth hardly becomes equitable if a larger fraction of the decline is concentrated at the top earners.

The Minimum Wage

The effort to promote equitable growth at the expense of the top 1 percent has serious consequences for current policy. It is no accident that in his recent State of the Union Address, President [Barack] Obama once again called for increases in taxes on "the wealthiest and the most powerful." If adopted, these changes would make the tax system more progressive and the economy more sluggish.

Indeed the President goes further. He pushes for the adoption of other wrong-headed policies that would also hurt the very people whom they are intended to help. Consider that the Lowrey story featured a picture of President Obama appearing before a crowd at the Linamar Corporation in Arden, N.C., seeking to make good on his promise to raise the minimum wage to $9.00—to advance, of course, the interests of the middle class to whom the President pays undying allegiance.

The President thinks he can redistribute income without stifling economic growth. The simple rules of supply and demand dictate that any increase in the minimum wage that expands the gap between the market wage and the statutory wage will increase the level of unemployment. The jobs that potential employees desperately need will disappear from the marketplace. In a weak economy, a jump in the minimum wage is likely, as the *Wall Street Journal* has noted, to reduce total jobs, with unskilled minority workers bearing the brunt of the losses.

All too often, the calls for equitable growth yield anything but the desired outcome.

Unfortunately, the President displays his resolute economic ignorance by proclaiming, "Employers may get a more stable workforce due to reduced turnover and increased productivity." But they can get that stability benefit unilaterally, without new legislation that throttles other employers for whom the proposition is false. Only higher productivity secures long-term higher wages.

A Better Solution

Indeed, the best thing the President could do is to just get out of the way. After over four years of his failed policies, [U.S. News & World Report publisher] Mortimer Zuckerman reports that unemployment rates still hover at 8 percent, and 6.4 million fewer people have jobs today than in 2007. That's an overall jobs decline of 4.9 percent in the face of a population growth of 12.5 million people from July 2007 to July of 2012. The same period has registered sharp increases in the number of people on disability insurance (to 11 million people) and food stamps (to some 48 million).

There is a deep irony in all of these dismal consequences. The President's State of the Union Address targeted the plight of the middle class. That appeal always makes political sense—

but it also makes for horrific economic policy. All too often, the calls for equitable growth yield anything but the desired outcome.

Rather than focus on "equitable growth," the President should focus on flattening the income tax and deregulating labor markets. Today's constant emphasis on progressive taxation and government intervention in labor markets will continue to lead the country, especially the middle class, on a downward path.

Inequality Does Not Make People Unhappy

Arthur C. Brooks

Arthur C. Brooks is president of the American Enterprise Institute and author of Gross National Happiness: Why Happiness Matters for America—And How We Can Get More of It.

May 13, 2009, at Arizona State University, Barack Obama delivered his first commencement address as President of the United States. At one of the most frightening economic moments in America's history, it was a chance to be a mentor, a teacher, and the nation's inspirer-in-chief.

Did the president urge the graduates to get out there and create the growth and jobs our country needs? Did he inspire them to be the next generation of great American innovators and entrepreneurs? No; instead, he told the graduates that people who "chase after all the usual brass rings" display "a poverty of ambition." He averred that this thinking "has been in our culture for far too long." He told them they could do better than trying "to be on this 'who's who' list or that top 100 list."

If you're a free marketeer, you've faced this charge a thousand times: You are a materialist. Meanwhile, your progressive interlocutors are interested in the higher-order things in life—such as fairness, compassion, and equality. Your vision for America might be wealthier, but theirs is happier.

Progressives have been making this case for generations. Their reasoning is clear. When people pursue "the usual brass rings" in the free market, there are winners, and there are losers. Many people get rich; many others do not. These differences may reflect merit and they may not. But one thing is for sure: Income inequality will result. And inequality, for many progressive leaders and intellectuals, is the enemy. In their view, it leads to an unjust, unhappy, Hobbesian [seventeenth-century English philosopher Thomas Hobbes, who believed a civil society depends on a sovereign authority and citizens should give up certain rights for the common good], all-against-all society.

A modern, compassionate society, they believe, can do better than the current system with its rising inequality. But that means employing more than soft rhetoric. We also need policies that weaken the free-enterprise system by lowering the rewards it brings to the winners as well as the consequences to the losers. As candidate Obama famously told Samuel Joseph Wurzelbacher—"Joe the Plumber"—on the campaign trail in October 2008, "I think when you spread the wealth around it's good for everybody."

Adherents to this philosophy believe that the best ways to meet their objectives are forced income redistribution, expansion of the state, or both. This is why the landmark policy initiatives of the past year—from health-care reform to financial-market regulation—have had bigger government and rising income redistribution at their core. Bureaucracy and taxes are not incidental to these policies, and not a mere cost of doing business; they are part of what many of our leaders seek to create and what they see as a better, fairer America.

It is factually incorrect to argue that income inequality has not risen in America—it has. The U.S. Census Bureau measures economic inequality through what is known as a Gini coefficient, which ranges from 0 to 1. Zero means no inequality (everyone has the same income) and 1 indicates perfect inequality (a single person has all the income). Between 1970 and 2005, the Gini coefficient in America increased by more than 20 percent, from 0.39 to 0.47.

As many progressives see it, this is a major problem, because inequality makes people unhappy. This argument has to be taken seriously, because, at first blush, the data appear to support it: Poorer people in almost every community tend to be unhappier than richer people. For example, the 2004 General Social Survey found that if you have an annual salary of less than $25,000, you are less than half as likely as someone earning more than $75,000 to describe yourself as "very happy."

> *A world defined by economic equality, the redistributionists believe, will be both a fairer and a happier one. And bringing the top down is every bit as good as bringing the bottom up, because greater equality is the goal.*

It doesn't even matter if you have plenty to get by in life. The evidence seems to show that simply having less than others makes you unhappy. This proposition was demonstrated in a famous experiment at Harvard University's School of Public Health in 1995. In it, a group of students and faculty were asked to choose between earning $50,000 per year while everyone else earned $25,000—or earning $100,000 per year while others made $200,000. The researchers stipulated that prices of goods and services would be the same in both cases, so a higher salary really meant being able to own a nicer home, buy a nicer car, or do whatever else they wanted with the extra money. However, the results showed that those materialistic perquisites mattered little to most people: Fifty-six percent chose the first option, hypothetically forgoing $50,000 per year simply to maintain a position of relative affluence.

Many have taken these results at face value: Inequality brings misery. That might be halfway acceptable to some if they thought inequality reflected differences in merit between people—in other words, if hard work and excellence were the primary explanation of why some people have more than others. But many progressives—even those who have done quite well themselves—reject this idea. Rather, they talk first and foremost about discrimination, luck, and exploitation. The 2005 Maxwell Poll on Civic Engagement and Inequality asked whether people agreed with the following statement: "While people may begin with different opportunities [in America], hard work and perseverance can usually overcome those disadvantages." Eight in ten Americans agreed, as well as more than nine in ten political conservatives.

Among those who disagreed, however, we find more than a third of political liberals with above-average incomes. For these progressive stalwarts, hard work and perseverance in America are useless when pitted against the faceless, amoral capitalist juggernaut. For those who believe this, of course, the only morally acceptable solution is to short-circuit free enterprise through forced equality. A world defined by economic equality, the redistributionists believe, will be both a fairer and a happier one. And bringing the top down is every bit as good as bringing the bottom up, because greater equality is the goal. Forced redistribution through taxation has other benefits, as well. It gets people out of the rat race for things they don't really need. They use fewer of the earth's resources and don't lord silly possessions over their neighbors. And with the taxes people pay, the government has more money to do all the good things governments can do.

Income equality is how redistributionists define the path to greater enlightenment and happiness for the rest of us. And that is why they are so willing to offer policies that sacrifice entrepreneurship for higher taxes, self-government for growing bureaucracies, individual achievement for powerful unions, and private businesses for federally managed corporations.

One problem with the redistributionists' approach is that it's based on a flawed premise—that greater income equality will bring us greater flourishing and happiness. A careful reading of the data demonstrates a crucially important truth, and one we overlook to our great peril: Inequality is not what makes people unhappy.

To understand this, we need to understand the concept of earned success. Earned success means the ability to create value through effort—not by winning the lottery, not by inheriting a fortune, and not by picking up a welfare check. It doesn't even mean making money itself. Earned success is the creation of value in our lives or the lives of others. It is what drives entrepreneurs to take risks, work hard, and make sacrifices. It is what parents get from raising happy children who are good people. It is the reward we enjoy when our time, money, and energy go to improving our world.

People who feel they have earned their success are much happier than people who feel they have not. In the working world—as opposed to, for example, lotteries   success is typically earned through effort. In 1996, the General Social Survey asked 500 American adults the following question: "How successful do you feel in your work life?" Some 45 percent answered "completely successful" or "very successful." The rest said that they were "somewhat successful" or less so. Among the first group, 39 percent said they were very happy in their lives. In the second group, just 20 percent said they were very happy.

The big problem is not that unhappy people have less money than others. It is that they have earned less success.

It turns out that this difference in happiness levels is not explained at all by differences in income. Imagine two people who are the same in income, as well as in education, age, sex, race, religion, politics, and family status. But one feels very successful, the other does not. The successful person will be about twice as likely as the other to report feeling "very happy" about his or her life. Similarly, the University of Michigan's Panel Study of Income Dynamics study asked several thousand people in 2001 whether they agreed or disagreed that they were responsible for their success. Those who "agreed" or "strongly agreed" with the statement spent 25 percent less time feeling sad than those who "disagreed" or "disagreed strongly" that they were responsible for their success.

Now, the self-described "completely successful" or "very successful" person may well be richer than the "somewhat successful" person, on average. That's because money frequently follows success in a capitalist system. But it's not the money that brings the feeling of success (and hence happiness). The money is just a metric of the value that the person is creating.

It's easy to confuse the two—money and earned success. But money is merely the symbol of earned success, important not primarily for what it can buy (although that's nice, too) but for what it says about how we are contributing, and the kind of difference we are making. That's why rich entrepreneurs continue to work so hard. They already have enough money to meet every need they could ever have. But they still crave earned success like the rest of us, and so they are driven to create more and more value. The economist Joseph Schumpeter—often called the godfather of modern entrepreneurship—said of entrepreneurs, "The financial result is a secondary consideration, or, at all events, mainly valued as an index of success and as a symptom of victory."

In a country such as the United States, where people are above the level of subsistence, a man of modest means who believes he has created something of value will tend to be much better off than a rich man who has not earned his success. The big problem is not that unhappy people have less money than others. It is that they have earned less success.

The way for the poor man to earn his success is through a system that rewards merit, hard work, education, and street smarts. It is through a system that matches skills and passions; that penalizes free-riding, laziness, and poor judgment. It is, in short, the free-enterprise system.

This finding is consistent with what many other social scientists have found in the past. Most notably, my AEI [American Enterprise Institute] colleague Charles Murray's seminal work in *Losing Ground* showed that the American welfare system before 1996 was a failure precisely because redistributed, unearned income could not solve the problems that plagued the poor.

An untrained observer of American society might be forgiven for thinking that the current debates about health care, financial-market regulation, and cap-and-trade are about economics. After all, the terms of the debate are taxes, government spending, and regulation of private profit-making activity. But in reality, these are part of America's new culture war, waged by many of our nation's political leaders and articulated by the president when he told college students that pursuing the "usual brass rings" had been part of our culture for far too long.

The truth is that free enterprise is not just a money machine—it is a happiness machine.

The discomfort so many Americans feel with the direction of our country is not due to the fact that our leaders' attacks on our free-enterprise system will lower economic-growth rates (although they most certainly will). The problem runs much deeper. People cherish free enterprise so much more than government because they know intuitively that it allows them to earn their success, and in turn to achieve the greatest levels of happiness.

This is why, even as the unemployment rate in the private sector soared in January 2010 and Wall Street scandals erupted, Gallup still found that six in ten Americans said they would prefer to work for business than for government (despite the fact that, on average, the government pays much better than the private sector). It is also why, when the Ayres-McHenry

113

company asked Americans during the depths of the recession in 2009, "Overall, would you prefer larger government with more services and higher taxes, or smaller government with fewer services and lower taxes?" Twenty-one percent favored the former, while 69 percent preferred the latter.

Free enterprise emphasizes creativity, meaning, optimism, and control of one's own life and seeks to escape from under the heavy hand of the state. It is traditional in its American values, yet perpetually new in its outlook. It naturally disdains the soul-sapping nature of Big Bureaucracy and the protected mediocrity of Big Labor, and has a healthy suspicion of the Faustian tendencies of Big Business—divorced from the entrepreneur's ethics—to crawl into bed with the government. In short, free enterprise is an act of self-expression—a declaration of what we truly value—and the ultimate "social issue" for Americans.

Americans may not naturally put free enterprise in such rhapsodic terms, which plays into redistributionists' sleight of hand in telling the electorate that free enterprise is just one economic alternative among many, and not a very fair one at that. The truth is that free enterprise is not just a money machine—it is a happiness machine. Conservatives are caught flat-footed if all they have to say about the administration's economic policies is that they are bad for efficiency.

To win the new culture war, the sizable majority in favor of free enterprise must claim the moral high ground. We must show that while we often use the language of commerce and business, what we really believe is that the purpose of free enterprise is the pursuit of happiness.

CHAPTER 3

Is the Wage Gap Among Races Problematic for Society?

Overview: Income by Race and Hispanic Origin

Carmen DeNavas-Walt, Bernadette D. Proctor, and Jessica C. Smith

Carmen DeNavas-Walt is statistician with the Income Statistics Branch, Bernadette D. Proctor with the Poverty Statistics Branch, and Jessica C. Smith with the Health and Disability Statistics Branch of the US Census Bureau.

Median household income was $50,054 in 2011, a 1.5 percent decline in real terms from 2010. This was the second consecutive annual decline in household income.

Changes in Household Income

In 2011, real median household income was 8.1 percent lower than in 2007, the year before the most recent recession, and was 8.9 percent lower than the median household income peak that occurred in 1999.

Median family household income declined by 1.7 percent in real terms between 2010 and 2011 to $62,273. The change in the median income of nonfamily households was not statistically significant.

Real median income declined for non-Hispanic-White households and Black households between 2010 and 2011, while the changes for Asian households and Hispanic households were not statistically significant.

Real median household incomes for each race and Hispanic-origin group have not yet recovered to their pre-2001 recession all-time highs.

Carmen DeNavas-Walt, Bernadette D. Proctor, and Jessica C. Smith, "Income in the United States," *Income, Poverty, and Health Insurance Coverage in the United States: 2011.* US Government Printing Office, 2012, pp 5, 7–9.

The real median incomes of households with a native-born householder and households maintained by a foreign-born naturalized citizen declined between 2010 and 2011. The change in the median income of households maintained by a noncitizen was not statistically significant.

The West experienced a decline in real median household income between 2010 and 2011, while the changes for the remaining regions were not statistically significant.

Income inequality between 2010 and 2011 increased as measured by changes in the shares of aggregate household income by quintiles, the Gini index, the Theil index, and the Atkinson measures [measures of income distribution]. The Gini index showed a 1.6 percent increase from 2010. This is the first time the Gini index has shown an annual increase since 1993, the earliest year available for comparable measures of income inequality. . . .

The Impact of Race and Hispanic Origin

Real median income declined for non-Hispanic-White households (by 1.4 percent) and Black households (by 2.7 percent) between 2010 and 2011. The changes for Asian and Hispanic-origin households were not statistically significant.

Real median household incomes for each of these groups have not yet recovered to their pre-2001 recession median household income peaks. Household income in 2011 was 7.0 percent lower for non-Hispanic Whites (from $59,604 in 1999), 16.8 percent lower for Blacks (from $38,747 in 2000), 10.6 percent lower for Asians (from $72,821 in 2000), and 10.8 percent lower for Hispanics (from $43,319 in 2000).

Among the race groups, Asian households had the highest median income in 2011 ($65,129). The median income was $55,412 for non-Hispanic-White households and $32,229 for Black households. For Hispanic households it was $38,624. Comparing the 2011 income of non-Hispanic-White households to that of other households shows that the ratio of

Asian to non-Hispanic-White income was 1.18, the ratio of Black to non-Hispanic-White income was 0.58, and the ratio of Hispanic to non-Hispanic-White income was 0.70. Between 1972 and 2011, the change in the Black-to-non-Hispanic-White income ratio was not statistically significant. Over the same period, the Hispanic-to-non-Hispanic-White income ratio declined from 0.74 to 0.70. Income data for the Asian population was first available in 1987. The 2011 Asian-to-non-Hispanic-White income ratio was not statistically different from the 1987 ratio.

Discrimination Explains the Low Wages of Black Men

Darrick Hamilton, Algernon Austin, and William Darity Jr.

Darrick Hamilton is associate professor of economics and urban policy at The New School for Public Engagement; Algernon Austin directs the Economic Policy Institute's Program on Race, Ethnicity and the Economy; and William Darity Jr. is professor of public policy in the Sanford School at Duke University.

In 2008, the year of the election of the nation's first black president, black men earned only 71% of what white men earned. In this report we examine how occupational segregation based on race is related to this disparity. We find that even after taking educational attainment into account, black men are overrepresented in low-wage jobs and underrepresented in high-wage jobs. Neither hard skills, soft skills, nor black men's occupational interests provide convincing explanations for black male sorting into low-wage occupations.

The most plausible explanation we find is that labor market discrimination excludes many black men from high-wage jobs. Therefore, effectively combating employment discrimination will contribute significantly to closing the racial earnings gap and improving the socioeconomic position of black families and black communities. . . .

A Racial Wage Gap

In 2008, the median hourly wage for black male full-time workers was $14.90, while the median for white male full-time workers was $20.84, nearly $6 higher. This wage disparity is not due primarily to differences in educational attainment between black and white men. Even when one looks at male full-time workers of the same educational level, one sees significant black-white wage disparities. Among workers with a high school diploma (or GED) or a bachelor's degree, black men earned only 74% of what white men earned.

One possible explanation for this wage disparity is that black men tend to be crowded into lower-paying occupations—even when they have similar educational attainment as white men. This theory of "occupational crowding" was put forth by [economist] Barbara Bergmann almost 40 years ago. She argued that black workers are denied employment in more desirable high-wage occupations and crowded into less-desirable low-wage occupations. The result is an oversupply of workers in the crowded occupations, which has the effect of lowering wages further in those jobs.

Bergmann states that employers' refusal to hire qualified black workers in desirable jobs may stem from their distaste for associating with blacks, misperceptions concerning the productivity of black workers, or a fear of negative reactions from their customers or current nonblack employees if black employees are hired. Even the black workers who are able to attain employment in white-dominant sectors receive relatively lower earnings than white workers because of the implicit threat that their only alternative is employment at even lower wages in sectors having an overrepresentation of black workers.

The analysis that follows uses data from the 2005–07 American Community Survey to explore the occupational crowding hypothesis. . . .

Segregated Workforces

In only 13% of all occupations are black men proportionally represented, thus 87% of U.S. occupations can be classified as segregated for black men. Black men are overrepresented in

38% of occupations and underrepresented in 49% of occupations.... The average of the annual wages in occupations in which black men are underrepresented is $50,533; the average in occupations in which they are overrepresented or occupationally crowded is $37,005, more than $13,000 less. Indeed, a statistical analysis reveals that a $10,000 increase in the average annual wage of an occupation is associated with a seven percentage-point decrease in the proportion of black men in that occupation.

More than half (54%) of management, professional, and related occupations have an underrepresentation of black men.

When this analysis is conducted within categories of occupations, we observe a pattern of black male exclusion from high-paying occupations and concentration in low-paying occupations....

Black males experience the most severe underrepresentation in construction, extraction, and maintenance occupations. This occupational sector is composed of 67 precisely defined occupations, and 81% of them are characterized by black male underrepresentation. These occupations tend to be low-educational-credential occupations; however, their wages tend to be higher than the wages for service occupations. Some of the annual earnings in the construction, extraction, and maintenance occupations also exceed annual earnings in production, transportation, and material moving occupations. Hence, these occupations present relatively desirable jobs for low-credentialed workers. Although black males are overrepresented among the distribution of low-credentialed workers, they are underrepresented in 81% of this comparatively desirable occupational sector.

The Management and Service Occupations

More than half (54%) of management, professional, and related occupations have an underrepresentation of black men. Management and professional occupations tend to require the highest educational credentials and offer the highest wages.

In the management and professional occupations, those jobs with an underrepresentation of black men have annual wages nearly $20,000 higher than the ones with an overrepresentation of black men ($68,684 versus $49,904). For these occupations, every $10,000 increase in occupational wages is associated with a nine percentage-point reduction in black male representation.

In contrast, black men are overrepresented in most of the service occupations. Similar to construction, extraction, and maintenance occupations, service occupations tend to have low degree requirements but, in contrast, they tend to offer low pay. Across all occupations the average occupational wage is $44,719, while the average occupational wage across all service occupations is considerably lower, $28,962. The average annual occupational wages in the 29 out of 53 (55%) service occupations in which blacks are overrepresented is only $25,552. Moreover, within this sector, we estimate that each $10,000 increase in the average occupational wage is associated with a 14 percentage-point reduction in black male representation.

> *In addition to relatively low wages, black men also suffer from a low employment rate.*

Underrepresentation and Overrepresentation

Sales and office occupations tend to have higher degree requirements than service occupations, yet we estimate a 14 percentage-point reduction in black male representation for a

$10,000 increase in occupational wages for this sector as well. . . . The 67% of sales and office occupations in which black males are overrepresented have average occupational wages that are $22,861 less than the 27% of occupations in which they are underrepresented ($34,790 versus $57,651).

Lastly, production, transportation, and material moving occupations are moderately credentialed occupations with the lowest degree of racial segregation. Nonetheless, more than 80% of these occupations are still segregated according to our measure. Indeed, this occupational sector has the strongest relationship between occupational wages and crowding scores. We estimate a 17 percentage-point reduction in the representation of black males in this sector for every $10,000 increase in the occupational wage.

Across occupational sectors, regardless of degree requirements, black males are underrepresented in high-wage occupations and overrepresented in low-wage occupations. We find a statistically significant correlation for this relationship for all occupations, and for all of the narrower occupational categories with the exception of the construction, extraction, and maintenance occupations. The lack of a relationship in the latter may be due to the low statistical power resulting from the high degree of exclusion of black men from these occupations in the first place. This issue is explored further in the following section.

Hard Facts Versus Soft Skills

In addition to relatively low wages, black men also suffer from a low employment rate. In recent years, scholars have argued that black men's supposed lack of soft skills is an important factor in explaining their difficulties in the labor market.

For example, [sociologist] William Julius Wilson argues that employers in service industries fail to hire black men because black men "lack the soft skills that their jobs require: the tendency to maintain eye contact, the ability to carry on polite and friendly conversations with consumers, the inclination to smile and be responsive to consumer requests." [Economist] Harry Holzer also puts forth weak soft skills as the culprit for limited upward mobility of black males, particularly young black males.

Service occupations, because they primarily involve serving customers, can be characterized as requiring relatively high levels of soft skills. In comparison, construction, extraction, and maintenance occupations, because they primarily involve working with materials and machinery, can be characterized as requiring relatively lower levels of soft skills.

Contrary to the arguments of Wilson, Holzer, and others, the empirical evidence put forth by [economist Sylvia] Allegretto and [labor-policy specialist Steven] Pitts and this current study does not support the soft-skills explanation for black male difficulties in the labor market. Allegretto and Pitts' analysis of the labor market by industry shows that black men are underrepresented in the construction and manufacturing industries but not in service industries. Thus, in service industries where soft skills are very important black men are well-represented or overrepresented. In construction and manufacturing industries, which have relatively low levels of soft-skill requirements, black men are underrepresented.

Our occupation-based analysis is consistent with Allegretto and Pitts' findings. The occupational category in which black men are most underrepresented is construction, extraction, and maintenance. On the other hand, the service occupations have the highest rate of occupational overrepresentation of black men. Again, this evidence is inconsistent with claims by Wilson, Holzer, and others that deficiencies in soft skills play a large role in explaining racial differences in labor market outcomes.

What the Data Show

Indeed, the underrepresentation of black men in construction, extraction, and maintenance occupations is extreme. There are

18 occupations in that category, and 27% have crowding scores below 0.50 (very high underrepresentation), but only 2–3% have crowding scores above 1.50 (very high overrepresentation). In contrast, in the service occupations only three occupations or 6% have scores under 0.50, but 20, or 38%, have scores over 1.50. While the highest crowding score in the construction, extraction, and maintenance occupations is 1.78 for hazardous materials removal workers, the highest in the service occupations is 3.64 for residential advisors, a position that presumably requires a strong set of soft skills. Thus, for construction, extraction, and maintenance occupations *in general*, there is a low representation of black men, while the opposite is true for service occupations.

Ultimately, it does not appear that either hard skills like educational attainment or soft skills explain the massive racial labor market disparities.

These data do not suggest that a lack of soft skills is responsible for black men's difficulties in the labor market. Black men have more success finding work in high soft-skills occupations like service work and sales and office occupations than in low soft-skills occupations like construction, extraction, and maintenance occupations and production, transportation, and material moving occupations.

Furthermore, . . . if black men were to move from the service sector occupations in which they are overrepresented to the construction, extraction, and maintenance occupations or the production, transportation, and material moving occupations, their wages would generally increase. Thus, rather than focusing on policies that promote the development of black male soft-skills, a more effective policy strategy might be aimed at moving blacks from lower-paying high-soft-skill service occupations to higher-paying low-soft-skill construction occupations.

Ultimately, it does not appear that either hard skills like educational attainment or soft skills explain the massive racial labor market disparities.

The Issue of Occupational Preferences

Given the relationship between black male representation and occupational wages across very different occupational categories, it seems unlikely that our results are driven by differences in the occupational preferences between black and white men. If, for example, black men prefer more physical work, which is more commonly found in the production, transportation, and material moving sector, and white men prefer less physical work, which is more commonly found in management, professional, and related occupations, then this might explain our findings across *all* occupations. After all, management, professional, and related occupations pay higher wages than production, transportation, and material moving occupations. But what would explain the results *within* occupational categories? Why would black men prefer lower wages within a given occupational sector?

The nation still remains challenged by a racially segregated workforce and labor market discrimination.

We offer a brief examination of racial differences in career choices to address the popular perception that bad career choices are basically responsible for racial differences in pay. Using college majors as an indicator of career preferences, we compare the college majors of black and white men. Although people often do not work in their major field of study, and college-degree recipients make up only a fraction of the entire labor force, we expect that, if there are big differences in black and white men's desired careers, they would manifest themselves in choices of majors. . . .

Overall, black and white men have a nearly identical distribution of college majors. . . .

Our examination of racial differences in college majors does not suggest that black male career choices are driving them to work in low-paying occupations. If left solely to their own desires, we would expect black and white men to have similar distributions of employment across and within occupational categories. This is especially true for management, professional, and related occupations, since these occupations typically require at least some college. . . .

Labor Market Discrimination

America is still racially segregated in the workplace. Even after accounting for educational attainment, black males are crowded into low-wage occupations and crowded out of high-wage occupations. We examined if these racial differences resulted from differences in occupational preferences, and whether they resulted from racial differences in the distribution of soft skills that are not captured by traditional measures of educational attainment. In neither case were we able to generate any substantial evidence that explained the disparate pattern of racial occupational sorting. In contrast, our analysis presents considerable evidence that is consistent with the finding, born out by audit study research, that identifies labor market discrimination as a mechanism for this sorting.

Much has been accomplished in the 40-plus years since the publication of Barbara Bergmann's seminal work on occupational segregation and the landmark passage of U.S. civil rights legislation. Blacks have held the highest positions in virtually every occupation in America, including president. Nonetheless, the nation still remains challenged by a racially segregated workforce and labor market discrimination, albeit less blatant than in our Jim Crow [racial segregation laws in the United States, 1876–1965] past.

Income Inequality Disproportionately Harms Women of Color

Sophia Kerby

Sophia Kerby is a policy associate at the Brennan Center for Justice at the New York University School of Law.

Today, April 9 [2013], is Equal Pay Day—the date that marks how many extra days women must work in 2013 to earn what men earned in 2012. Unfortunately, the wages of working women and particularly the wages of women of color continue to lag behind the pay of their male counterparts. Moreover, for women of color there is a double pay gap. As a group, women of color earn less than their white female peers—a reality that means they need to work longer to earn the same pay as white women and then even longer to match the earnings of white men. The gender- and race-based wage gap affects families of color with long-term consequences that hinder wealth accumulation.

Women currently make up about half of all workers in the U.S. labor force and among mothers in the labor force the majority are either breadwinners or share that responsibility with a partner. In 2010, 13.1 percent of women in the workforce were black, 4.7 percent were Asian, and 12.8 percent were Latina. What's more, these women of color are increasingly the breadwinners in their families—53.3 percent of black households and 40.1 percent of Latino households.

This issue brief will examine our nation's gender-based wage gap and its racial overlay. It will look specifically at the long-term implications of the wage gap on communities of color and then suggest policy recommendations to narrow and eventually eliminate the wage gap to ensure equal work earns equal pay.

The Wage and Income Gap

The gender-based wage gap disproportionately hurts women of color who have made less than their white counterparts for decades. Women of color are more likely to work in lower-paying jobs and experience higher levels of unemployment and poverty.

Women on average earn 77 cents for every dollar a man earns for comparable work—a gender wage gap of 23 percent. Women of color suffer from an even more severe gap. According to the National Partnership for Women and Families, African American women and Latinas in the United States are paid $18,817 and $23,298 less than non-Hispanic white men yearly, respectively. That's 64 cents and 55 cents for every dollar a man earns.

The gender gap persists for median weekly earnings as well. Women's median weekly earnings in 2012 were $691, a marginal decline compared to 2011. Men's median weekly earnings were $854, a marginal increase compared to 2011. Women of all major racial and ethnic groups earn less than men of the same group. The largest gap is within Asian American communities where women earn a median weekly income of $770 compared to $1,055 for Asian American men. While the wage gap between men and women is smaller within Latino and black families, their median weekly earnings are significantly lower. The weekly median earnings for Latinas are $521 compared to $592 for Latino men. For black women, their weekly earnings are $599 compared to $665 for black men. African American women's median weekly earnings were only 68.1 percent, and Latina women's only 59.3 percent of median weekly white men's earnings of $854.

Nearly half of the wage gap between men and women is due to differences in occupations because women are concentrated in industries such as the care and social services sectors that historically pay less and provide fewer benefits. Another 10 percent of the gender wage gap is due to differences in work experience between men and women, which are often the result of caretaking responsibilities. Often times workers with care responsibilities, usually women, withdraw from the workforce or limit their time at work to allow them to provide needed care at home. As a consequence these caretakers earn less income in the short run, are less likely to earn raises and promotions, have less access to workplace retirement benefits, earn less in Social Security retirement benefits, and accumulate lower lifetime earnings.

Closing the pay gap is even more important for women of color who are more likely than their white counterparts to be breadwinners.

Yet even when controlling for occupational differences, experience, and education level, economists cannot explain the remaining 40 percent of the wage gap between men and women. Certainly part of the gender gap is due to the fact that the American workplace and institutions, such as schools and churches, never adjusted to support working families. A lack of flexible structures for working families forces them to make tough decisions. Schools that do not offer early drop-off or late pick-up options to parents, for example, force families to decide between missing work or paying for child care. For low-income families, such decisions could mean losing a job.

The Long-Term Implications of the Wage Gap

Lower income for all women, particularly those of color, means less money to support their families with necessities such as housing, food, education, and health care. Closing the pay gap is even more important for women of color who are more likely than their white counterparts to be breadwinners.

The long-term wage gap hurts families of color tremendously, forcing families to choose between putting food on the table or saving for a college education and retirement. On average, an African American woman working full time loses the equivalent of 118 weeks of food each year due to the wage gap. A Latina loses 154 weeks' worth of food. The stubbornly persistent gender-based wage gap adds up substantially over the lifetime of a woman's career. For women of color the loss of savings over a 30-hour-a-week to a 40-hour-a-week work lifespan is significant. A woman of color will have to live on one-third to 45 percent less than a white man based on the average benefits that are afforded through Social Security and pension plans. Research shows that a woman's average lifetime earnings are more than $434,000 less than a comparable male counterpart over a 35-year working life.

Analysis done in 2012 by the Center for American Progress [CAP] illustrates that the money lost over the course of a working woman's lifetime could do one of the following:

- Feed a family of four for 37 years

- Pay for seven four-year degrees at a public university

- Buy two homes

- Purchase 14 new cars

- Simply be saved for retirement and used to boost her quality of life when she leaves the workforce

Lifetime earnings are even lower for women of color because they face higher levels of unemployment and poverty rates. In March 2013 unemployment rates of black and Latina women were significantly higher than their white counterparts at 12.2 percent and 9.3 percent respectively compared to white women at 6.1 percent. According to the National Women's

Law Center, poverty rates among women, particularly women of color, remain historically high and unchanged in the last year. The poverty rate among women was 14.6 percent in 2011—the highest in the last 18 years. For black and Latina women that same year, the poverty rate was 25.9 percent and 23.9 percent, respectively.

The Pay Gap Among Millennials

Furthermore, the gender wage gap often starts right out of college. The American Association of University Women reports that women are less likely than men to be fully employed in their first year out of college. When they do have a steady job, women earn less, adding to the burden of student loan debt. In fact, Millennial women—those born between 1978 and 2000—are paid 82 cents for every dollar paid to their male peers, and young women contribute a larger portion of their salaries to repaying student loans.

Millennial women of color are particularly impacted by the wage gap starting right out of college.

In 2009, 47 percent of young women were paying more than 8 percent of their income toward student loan debt one year after graduation. For Millennial men, only 39 percent were contributing more than 8 percent of their income to paying off their student debt.

These income disparities so early in a woman's career create financial barriers that prevent women from obtaining the same types of economic advantages that are available to their male counterparts such as purchasing a house or saving for retirement. Women are losing out financially from their very first paycheck. Even when controlling for factors such as the type of degree earned, type of occupation right out of college, and hours worked in that job, researchers found a significant pay discrepancy across the board between Millennial women and men.

Millennial women of color are particularly impacted by the wage gap starting right out of college. Even while more women than men of color are graduating from college, the impact of student loans exacerbates the gender-based wage gap. From 2009 to 2010 black females earned 68 percent of associate's degrees and 66 percent of bachelor's degrees awarded to African American students. Hispanic females earned 62 percent of associate's degrees and 61 percent of bachelor's degrees awarded to Hispanic students. Since women of color are more likely to attend college within their communities, the amount of student debt that young students of color take out disproportionately impacts them. In the 2007–08 academic year, 81 percent of African Americans and 67 percent of Latinos with a bachelor's degree graduated with student debt compared to 64 percent of their white peers. Although women of color are making progress in closing the achievement gap within their racial and ethnic groups, the impact of student debt on the wage gap right out of college puts women of color in a vulnerable state.

The Barriers to Wealth Accumulation

Pay discrepancy often hinders wealth accumulation and creates barriers to moving into the middle class. Such income disparities translate into wealth gaps that fall particularly heavily on those living at the intersection of gender and race. Lower earnings mean fewer opportunities to participate in wealth-building mechanisms such as investments in stocks and bonds and pension plans. Access to these opportunities is often unavailable in low-paying jobs that are predominantly held by women of color. According to the Bureau of Labor Statistics, black and Latino women were significantly more likely than their white counterparts to be among the working poor—those who are employed whose incomes fall below the federal poverty line. The working-poor rates for black and Latino women in 2011 were 14.5 percent and 13.8 percent respectively compared to white women who had a working-poor rate of 6.6 percent.

Immigrant women face specific economic barriers that make them the least economically secure population in the United States and puts them at a unique disadvantage.

Closing the wage gap is crucial for women of color. The racial wealth differences in the United States are consequences of disparities occurring over a lifetime and result in a median wealth of only $5 for women of color between the ages of 35 to 49—virtually no wealth at all. Conversely, white women in that age cohort have a median wealth of $42,600, and white men in that age group enjoy a median wealth of $70,030. While earnings are important in accumulating wealth, other factors play a significant role in building wealth including paid sick leave, health insurance, pensions, and 401(k) plans. Over time the lack of equitable pay prevents women of color from taking advantage of wealth-building resources that act as a buffer to potential financial setbacks such as a health emergency, a death in the family, or temporary unemployment.

As women's earnings continue to become increasingly important to families, closing the gender-based wage gap is crucial to gaining access to wealth accumulation in communities of color, which are still deprived of economic security.

The Impact on Immigrant Women

Immigrant women face specific economic barriers that make them the least economically secure population in the United States and puts them at a unique disadvantage. These barriers include the realities of having language and cultural barriers, the complexity of their immigration status, the responsibility of caring for extended family members, working in low-paying jobs, and lacking eligibility for many public benefit programs.

There are approximately 4 million undocumented immigrant women living and working in the United States, but because of their immigration status, they work the lowest-paying jobs in the country. Undocumented immigrant women typically earn minimum wage or less, get no sick leave or vacation days, and receive no health insurance. Undocumented immigrant Mexican women face hourly wage disparity of 71 cents. Pay equity is often a lifeline for immigrant women since many are mothers and are most likely to support family members in their home countries.

Immigrant women, especially those who are undocumented, are especially susceptible to abuse in the workplace as they work in low-paying jobs with no benefits and have little access to public-benefit programs. Since immigrant women predominantly work in the domestic workforce, they face a host of barriers to achieving pay equity in the workforce.

Immigrants comprise 46 percent of the domestic workforce and almost the entire population of domestic workers in major cities such as New York. A study by Domestic Workers United found that 33 percent of domestic workers in New York City experienced some form of physical or verbal abuse, often because of their race or immigration status. Under these conditions immigrant women struggle to achieve pay equity against the numerous barriers put up against them such as language and cultural barriers, immigration status, and concentration in low-income jobs with limited benefits.

The Impact on Lesbian Women of Color

Lesbian women of color struggle even more with issues of pay inequity, high poverty, unemployment rates, and discrimination. Working gay and transgender people of color still earn less than their heterosexual and white gay and transgender counterparts, but lesbian women of color struggle even more severely. The average Latina lesbian couple earns $3,000 less than Latino opposite-sex couples. Black lesbian couples face an even greater economic disparity earning $10,000 less than black same-sex male couples. Black same-sex couples significantly lag behind white same-sex couples with median incomes of $41,500 compared to $63,500.

Furthermore, lesbian couples of color experience high rates of poverty and unemployment. In 2012 the poverty rate for black lesbian couples was 21.1 percent; for Latina lesbian couples the rate, was 19.1 percent; for Native American lesbian couples, the rate was 13.7 percent; and for Asian Pacific Islander lesbian couples, it was 11.8 percent. These numbers stand in stark contrast to white lesbian couples who had poverty rates of only 4.3 percent.

Pay equity is imperative for lesbian couples of color who are more likely to have children than their white counterparts. An estimated 2 million children are being raised in gay, lesbian, and transgender families who tend to be more racially and ethnically diverse. In fact 46.7 percent of black lesbian couples and 41.5 percent of Latina lesbian couples are raising children compared to 23.1 percent of white lesbian couples. These families suffer when household incomes are unjustly decreased based on gender-, race-, and sexual orientation-wage bias.

As families continue to rely on women to contribute to household income and support their families, closing the wage gap for all women and in particular women of color is an imperative.

The Effect of Closing the Wage Gap

The disparity in income adds up to more than $430,000 in lost wages for an individual woman and even more for a woman of color over her working life. This means less food on the table, less in savings for retirement and medical emergency, less money going toward a college education for their children to name just a few of the negative financial impacts. If the wage gap were closed today, a working black woman with her increased yearly pay could afford one of the following:

- Groceries for more than two years

- Mortgage and utilities payments for almost 10 months

- Rent on an apartment for more than 16 months of rent

- Health insurance premiums for more than three years

- 4,549 additional gallons of gas

Furthermore, women breadwinners are on the rise among all races and ethnicities. From 1975 to 2010 black and Latina women nearly doubled in percentage of working wives who are earning the same or more than their spouses. Among black families, 53.3 percent of women are breadwinners, up from 45.7 percent in 2007 and 28.7 percent in 1975. For Latino and white families in 2010, about 4 in 10 working wives are breadwinners—nearly double their rates from 1975.

As families continue to rely on women to contribute to household income and support their families, closing the wage gap for all women and in particular women of color is an imperative.

Some Policy Suggestions and Recommendations

The gender wage gap doesn't just hurt women; it also hurts families. With nearly two-thirds of mothers being breadwinners or sharing the responsibilities of supporting the household, women's paychecks are vital to families more than ever.

Below are CAP's suggested recommendations and policy solutions to significantly reduce the pay equity gap among women of color:

- *Support the Paycheck Fairness Act.* Sen. Barbara Mikulski (D-MD) and Rep. Rosa DeLauro (D-CT) co-sponsored the Paycheck Fairness Act, which will require that an employer justify paying a man more than a woman for the same job. It would also make it easier for women to file class action suits against their employers for alleged sex-based discrimination. Though the bill failed to pass in 2011 and 2012, it was reintroduced this year [2013].

- *Pass legislation to support paid sick and family medical leave.* According to CAP's paid family and medical leave report, federally required paid family and medical leave programs will likely have positive effects on employment and lifetime income. Requiring employers to provide sick leave not only ensures workers' rights, but it will also help lessen gender-based pay disparities since women are more likely to use unpaid sick leave to care for their children.

Adequately addressing and eventually eliminating the income and wealth gap experienced by women of color requires a multifaceted approach led by engagement at both the state and federal level. As women's earnings become increasingly important to family incomes, the wage gap becomes a family issue. Promoting and uplifting women of color is crucial to growing our economy. Ensuring that all working women, and particularly women of color, receive fair wages for their work not only means that they can adequately provide for themselves and their families, but also means they can make an even greater contribution to the nation's prosperity.

The Racial Wage Gap Contributes to a Racial Wealth Gap

Signe-Mary McKernan et al.

In addition to Signe-Mary McKernan, the following viewpoint was written by Caroline Ratcliffe, Eugene Steuerle, and Sisi Zhang. McKernan and Ratcliffe are senior fellows, Steuerle is Richard B. Fisher chair and institute fellow, and Zhang is a research associate at the Urban Institute.

Policymakers often focus on income and overlook wealth, but consider: the racial wealth gap is three times larger than the racial income gap. Such great wealth disparities help explain why many middle-income blacks and Hispanics haven't seen much improvement in their relative economic status and, in fact, are at greater risk of sliding backwards.

The Racial Wealth Gap

Wealth is not just for the wealthy. The poor can have wealth too—and that wealth can accrue over time or provide collateral for borrowing, giving families a way to move up and out of poverty. A home or a car can offer benefits far beyond their cash value. And even a small amount of savings can help families avoid falling into a vicious cycle of debt when a job loss or financial emergency hits.

Wealth disparities have worsened over the past 30 years. High-wealth families (the top 20 percent by net worth) saw their average wealth increase by nearly 120 percent between 1983 and 2010, while middle-wealth families saw their average wealth go up by only 13 percent. The lowest-wealth families—

Signe-Mary McKernan, Caroline Ratcliffe, Eugene Steuerle, and Sisi Zhang, "Less Than Equal: Racial Disparities in Wealth Accumulation," Urban Institute, April 2013, pp. 1–5. Reproduced by permission.

those in the bottom 20 percent—saw their average wealth fall well below zero, meaning their average debts exceed their assets.

There is extraordinary wealth inequality between the races. In 2010, whites on average had six times the wealth of blacks and Hispanics. So for every $6.00 whites had in wealth, blacks and Hispanics had $1.00 (or average wealth of $632,000 versus $103,000).

The income gap, by comparison, is much smaller. In 2010, the average income for whites was twice that of blacks and Hispanics ($89,000 versus $46,000), meaning that for every $2.00 whites earned, blacks and Hispanics earned $1.00.

How have these two measures changed over time? Neither has improved, but while the income gap has stayed roughly the same, the wealth gap has grown. In 1983, the average wealth of whites was roughly five times that of blacks and Hispanics.

In inflation-adjusted 2010 dollars, as opposed to ratios, the gap is also growing—as would happen in any growing economy if the ratios remained constant, much less moved farther apart. The average wealth of white families was $230,000 higher than the average wealth of black and Hispanic families in 1983. By 2010, the average wealth of white families was over a half-million dollars higher than the average wealth of black and Hispanic families ($632,000 versus $98,000 and $110,000, respectively). If we look at the median family the wealth holdings are lower and the differences are smaller, but the trends are the same.

The Wealth Gap Over Time

The racial wealth gap grows sharply with age. Early in wealth-building years (when adults are in their 30s), white families have 3.5 to 4 times the wealth of families of color. Over the life cycle these initial racial differences grow in both absolute and relative terms.

Whites on average are on a higher accumulation curve than blacks or Hispanics. Whites age 32–40 in 1983 had an average family wealth of $184,000. In 2010, near their peak wealth-building years of age 59–67, average white family wealth had shot up to $1.1 million. In contrast, blacks age 32–40 in 1983 saw their average family wealth rise more slowly, from $54,000 to $161,000 by 2010. Meanwhile, average family wealth for Hispanics increased from $46,000 in 1983 to $226,000 in 2010. In other words, whites in this cohort started with about three and a half times more wealth than blacks in their 30s but had seven times more wealth in their 60s. Compared with Hispanics, whites started with four times more wealth in their 30s but had nearly five times more wealth three decades later.

While the Great Recession didn't cause the wealth disparities between whites and minorities, it did exacerbate them.

Blacks especially, but also Hispanics, are not on the same compound growth path. Particularly important, these families of color are less likely to own homes and have retirement accounts than whites, so they miss out on the automatic behavioral component of these traditionally powerful wealth-building vehicles. In 2010, fewer than half of black and Hispanic families owned homes, while three-quarters of white families did.

The Impact of the Great Recession

While the Great Recession didn't cause the wealth disparities between whites and minorities, it did exacerbate them. The 2007–09 recession brought about sharp declines in the wealth of white, black, and Hispanic families alike, but Hispanics experienced the largest decline. Lower home values account for much of Hispanics' wealth loss, while retirement accounts are where blacks were hit hardest.

Between 2007 and 2010, Hispanic families saw their wealth cut by over 40 percent, and black families saw their wealth fall by 31 percent. By comparison, the wealth of white families fell by 11 percent.

Like a lot of young families, many Hispanic families bought homes just before the recession. Because they started with higher debt-to-asset values, the sharp decline in housing prices meant an even sharper cut in Hispanics' wealth. As a result, they were also more likely to end up underwater or with negative home equity. Between 2007 and 2010, Hispanics saw their home equity cut in half, compared with about a quarter for black and white families.

In contrast, black families lost the most in retirement assets, while white families experienced a slight increase. On average, blacks saw their retirement assets fall by 35 percent during the Great Recession, compared with a smaller (but still substantial) decline of 18 percent for Hispanic families. This finding is consistent with research that suggests lower-income families are more likely to withdraw money from retirement savings after a job loss or other adverse event. The high rates of unemployment and other financial needs that took hold with the Great Recession appear to have led to larger declines in retirement savings for black families.

Because Hispanics and blacks are disproportionately low income, their wealth building is strongly affected by policies aimed at low-income families.

The stock market has essentially recovered since the recession. So, those families able to hold onto their retirement saving over longer periods (such as those who remain employed or have other assets to which they can turn) come out much better than those who sell when markets are low.

The Need for Reformed Policies

Families of color were disproportionately affected by the recession. However, the fact that they were not on good wealth-building paths before this financial crisis calls into question whether a whole range of policies (from tax to safety net) have actually been helping minorities get ahead in the modern economy. More fundamentally, it raises the question of whether social welfare policies pay too little attention to wealth building and mobility relative to consumption and income.

Because Hispanics and blacks are disproportionately low income, their wealth building is strongly affected by policies aimed at low-income families. Right now, safety net policies emphasize consumption: the Supplemental Nutrition Assistance Program and Temporary Assistance for Needy Families, for example, try to ensure that families have enough food to eat and other basic necessities. Many safety net programs even discourage saving: families can become ineligible if they have a few thousand dollars in savings. Wealth-building policies, on the other hand, are delivered as tax subsidies for homeownership and retirement. Since families of color are less likely to be able to use these subsidies, they benefit little or not at all.

Most families save by paying off mortgages through home-ownership and accumulating wealth in compounding retirement accounts. The automatic component of these assets—a monthly mortgage payment, regular deposits from earnings to savings—facilitate wealth building. Both methods are threatened by some disturbing current trends. The Great Recession led many low-income individuals to fear homeownership even when it became much cheaper on net than renting. Meanwhile mortgage credit has tightened—and might be further tightened with higher down payment rates—making credit most available in a bubble market and least in a bust market. For low-income families, especially families of color, this can exacerbate wealth inequality. Retirement savings, meanwhile, are threatened as a result of reduced employer contributions to pension plans and early employee withdrawals.

A common misconception is that poor or even low-income families cannot save. Research and evidence from savings programs shows they can. When we examined families living below the poverty level, we found that over a decade more than 40 percent were able to increase their net worth and save enough to escape asset poverty—in other words, they had enough assets to live at the poverty level for three months without income (about $3,000 for an individual and $6,000 for a family of four).

The federal government spends hundreds of billions of dollars each year to support long-term asset development. But these asset-building subsidies primarily benefit high-income families, while low-income families receive next to nothing. Reforming policies like the mortgage interest tax deduction so it benefits all families, and helping families enroll in automatic savings vehicles, will help improve wealth inequality and promote saving opportunities for all Americans.

Discrimination Does Not Explain the Race and Gender Wage Gaps

June O'Neill

June O'Neill is Wollman Distinguished Professor of Economics and director of the Center for the Study of Business and Government at Zicklin School of Business at Baruch College in New York City.

With Equal Pay Day on April 9 [2013] and the *Fisher v. University of Texas at Austin* affirmative action case pending in the US Supreme Court, gender- and race-based discrimination continues to simmer in public discourse. The debates over competing views of the scope and causes of these wage gaps raise key questions for federal employment policy. Are wage gaps created by predatory employers, or do gaps reflect differences in work experience, cognitive strengths, and choice of occupations and work settings? And what reforms should policymakers pursue to address the roots of these gaps?

Lost in the hand wringing and the call for more stringent government action are the facts that show considerable economic progress for minorities and women over the years. In 1940, the average weekly wage of adult black men was only 45% as much as that of white men. Over the next 20 years—a period with little or no federal anti-discrimination policy—the wage ratio increased to 61%. That change was accomplished through relative gains in the education of African Americans, combined with the mass migration of blacks out of the South to other parts of the country where wages were

June O'Neill, "Race and Gender Wage Gaps: Discrimination Still to Blame?" *AEIdeas*, April 9, 2013. Reprinted with permission from the AEIdeas blog (www.aei-ideas.org), a publication of the American Enterprise Institute, Washington, DC.

higher and discrimination less pervasive. Between 1960 and 1980, progress continued and the wage ratio rose to 75%, aided by the passage of Title VII of the Civil Rights Act. The wage gains of black women were even more striking, starting from a black-white ratio of 41% in 1940, rising to 66% in 1960 and to 96% in 1980.

Although African Americans have gone on to gain distinction in many fields, there has been little change in these overall ratios since 1980. Some groups attribute the stagnation of the male racial wage gap to persistent racism. But many economists point to changes in the economy over the past 25 years that have led to wage premiums for high-level cognitive skills. Among all groups there has been increasing inequality tied to skills acquired in higher levels of schooling and especially in fields such as engineering, science, and finance. For a variety of reasons, blacks enter the labor force with lower cognitive skills than whites. For example, black college-bound students score about 100 points lower on the various components of the SAT than white students. Studies have found that the pay gap between white and black workers is fully explained when differences in scores on tests of cognitive skills such as the AFQT (Armed Forces Qualifications Test) are included as part of the analysis. In other words, black and white workers with similar educational background and test scores are found to have similar earnings. Notably, and consistent with the wage premium for high skills, some non-white minorities, notably those of Asian origin, are among the highest-paid workers in the United States. They are also among the most highly educated groups in the economy.

What about the gender gap in wages? In 1960, the ratio of women's earnings to men's was 59% and it remained at about that level through the 60's and 70's. The stagnation of the ratio attracted the ire of the growing women's movement and inspired a button memorializing the 59% gap. The ratio had seemingly been immune to the Civil Rights Act of 1964 and the growth of federal anti-discrimination measures. But the gap began to narrow quite rapidly in the 1980s as women acquired more years of continuous work experience and more pertinent work preparation. In 2011, the labor department reported a gender wage ratio of 81%.

In today's world, employer discrimination is not an important reason for either the race or gender gap in pay.

The gender wage gap, unlike the racial wage gap, is mainly related to choices that women make between home and the workplace. Working women typically have had as much education as male workers. In fact, in recent years women have been acquiring more years of education than men, particularly at the post graduate level, and that education gives them greater access to relatively high-paying occupations. But women also value time spent with their children and as a consequence are more likely to work part-time, to take more career breaks than men, and therefore to accumulate fewer years of continuous work experience. Occupations and job situations that allow for part-time work and convenient schedules pay less. For reasons such as these, childless women who never marry earn more than married women and as much as similarly situated men.

Studies that adjust for such factors as differences in work experience and job demands find little if any gender pay gap. Nonetheless, women's advocacy organizations continue to call for legislation that would directly impose measures to close the gap. The most recent example is the Paycheck Fairness Act, which has failed to garner the votes needed for passage. A particular call to arms of women's groups is the fact that only a small percentage of women reach the "top." But should society do something to push women into aiming for high level, high paying executive jobs that would limit time spent with children while evening the difference in the sexes? Sheryl

Sandberg, author of the best seller "Lean In" and herself a COO [chief operating officer] of Facebook, urges us to move in that direction. But do we know enough about the value of mother-provided childcare and the losses that might emerge?

In today's world, employer discrimination is not an important reason for either the race or gender gap in pay. But what useful role then can there be for federal anti-discrimination policy? The passage of Title VII of the Civil Rights Act led to the dismantling of the open segregation that was entrenched in the South with significant effects on the earnings and job opportunities of African Americans. But in the ensuing decades, the activities of the federal agencies charged with implementation have not had any perceptible positive effects. In fact, the Office of Federal Contract Compliance (OFCCP), in a vain attempt to engineer equal outcomes, imposes racial and gender quotas on federal contractors. Yet Title VII called for equality of opportunity and outlawed the implementation of quotas. It is time to rescind the Executive Order that sustains the OFCCP.

Minimum Wage Laws Hurt, Not Help, Unskilled Black Youths

Walter E. Williams

Walter E. Williams is the John M. Olin Distinguished Professor of Economics at George Mason University and a syndicated columnist.

As if more proof were needed about the minimum wage's devastating effects, yet another study has reached the same conclusion. Last week [May 5, 2011], two labor economists, Professors William Even (Miami University of Ohio) and David Macpherson (Trinity University), released a study for the Washington, D.C.-based Employment Policies Institute titled "Unequal Harm: Racial Disparities in the Employment Consequences of Minimum Wage Increases."

The Unemployment Rate of Young Black Men

During the peak of what has been dubbed the Great Recession, the unemployment rate for young adults (16 to 24 years of age) as a whole rose to above 27 percent. The unemployment rate for black young adults was almost 50 percent, but for young black males, it was 55 percent.

Even and Macpherson say that it would be easy to say this tragedy is an unfortunate byproduct of the recession, but if you said so, you'd be wrong. Their study demonstrates that increases in the minimum wage at both the state and federal level are partially to blame for the crisis in employment for minority young adults.

Walter E. Williams, "Minimum Wage's Discriminatory Effects," Townhall.com, May 11, 2011. Copyright © 2011 by Walter E. Williams. All rights reserved. Reproduced by permission.

Their study focuses on 16-to-24-year-old male high school dropouts, understandably a relatively inexperienced group of labor market participants. Since minimum wage laws discriminate against the employment of the least-skilled worker, it shouldn't be surprising to find 16-to-24-year-old male high school dropouts its primary victims.

Among the white males, the authors find that "each 10 percent increase in a state or federal minimum wage has decreased employment by 2.5 percent; for Hispanic males, the figure is 1.2 percent.

"But among black males in this group, each 10 percent increase in the minimum wage decreased employment by 6.5 percent."

The authors go on to say, "The effect is similar for hours worked: each 10 percent increase reduces hours worked by 3 percent among white males, 1.7 percent for Hispanic males, and 6.6 percent for black males."

The Effect of the Minimum Wage

Even and Macpherson compare the job loss caused by higher minimum wages with that caused by the recession and find between 2007 and 2010, employment for 16-to-24-year-old black males fell by approximately 34,300 as a result of the recession; over the same time period, approximately 26,400 lost their jobs as a result of increases in the minimum wage across the 50 states and at the federal level.

Why do young black males suffer unequal harm from minimum wage increases? Even and Macpherson say that they're more likely to be employed in low-skilled jobs in eating and drinking establishments. These are businesses with narrow profit margins and are more adversely affected by increases in minimum wage increases. For 16-to-24-year-old men without a high school diploma, 25 percent of whites and 31 percent of blacks work at an eating and drinking establishment. Compounding the discriminatory burden of minimum wages, not discussed by the authors, are the significant educational achievement differences between blacks and whites.

The best way to sabotage chances for upward mobility of a youngster from a single-parent household, who resides in a violent slum and has attended poor-quality schools is to make it unprofitable for any employer to hire him. The way to accomplish that is to mandate an employer to pay such a person a wage that exceeds his skill level.

Imagine that a worker's skill level is such that he can only contribute $5 worth of value per hour to the employer's output, but the employer must pay him a minimum wage of $7.25 per hour, plus mandated fringes such as Social Security, unemployment compensation and health insurance. To hire such a worker would be a losing economic proposition. If the employer could pay that low-skilled worker the value of his skills, he would at least have a job and a chance to upgrade his skill and earn more in the future.

Minimum wage laws have massive political support, including that of black politicians. That means that many young black males will remain a part of America's permanent underclass with crime, drugs and prison as their future.

CHAPTER 4

Is Education Key to Reducing Wage Gaps?

Education Is the Key to a Healthy Economy

George P. Shultz and Eric A. Hanushek

George P. Shultz is a former US secretary of state and currently the Thomas W. and Susan D. Ford Distinguished Fellow at the Hoover Institution at Stanford University. Eric A. Hanushek is the Paul and Jean Hanna Senior Fellow at the Hoover Institution.

In addressing our current fiscal and economic woes, too often we neglect a key ingredient of our nation's economic future—the human capital produced by our K-12 school system. An improved education system would lead to a dramatically different future for the U.S., because educational outcomes strongly affect economic growth and the distribution of income.

Over the past half century, countries with higher math and science skills have grown faster than those with lower-skilled populations. . . . We compare GDP-per-capita growth rates between 1960 and 2000 with achievement results on international math assessment tests. The countries include almost all of the Organization for Economic Cooperation and Development (OECD) countries plus a number of developing countries. What stands out is that all the countries follow a nearly straight line that slopes upward—as scores rise, so does economic growth. Peru, South Africa and the Philippines are at the bottom; Singapore and Taiwan, the top.

The U.S. growth rate lies above the line because—despite the more recent shortcomings of our schools—we've long benefited from our commitment to the free movement of labor and capital, strong property rights, a limited degree of government intrusion in the economy, and strong colleges and universities. But each of these advantages has eroded considerably and should not be counted on to keep us above the line in the future.

Current U.S. students—the future labor force—are no longer competitive with students across the developed world. In the OECD's Programme for International Student Assessment (PISA) rankings for 2009, the U.S. was 31st in math— indistinguishable from Portugal or Italy. In "advanced" performance on math, 16 countries produced twice as many high achievers per capita than the U.S. did.

If we fail to reform our K-12 education system, we'll be locking in inequality problems that will plague us for decades if not generations to come.

If we accept this level of performance, we will surely find ourselves on a low-growth path.

This doesn't have to be our fate. Imagine a school improvement program that made us competitive with Canada in math performance (which means scoring approximately 40 points higher on PISA tests) over the next 20 years. As these Canadian-skill-level students entered the labor force, they would produce a faster-growing economy.

How much faster? The results are stunning. The improvement in GDP over the next 80 years would exceed a present value of $70 trillion. That's equivalent to an average 20% boost in income for every U.S. worker each year over his or her entire career. This would generate enough revenue to solve easily the U.S. debt problem that is the object of so much current debate.

The drag on growth is by no means the only problem produced by our lagging education system. Greater educational disparity leads to greater income-distribution disparity. If we fail to reform our K-12 education system, we'll be locking in inequality problems that will plague us for decades if not generations to come.

Take our own state of California. Once a leader in education, it is now ranked behind 40 other U.S. states in math achievement, placing it at the level of Greece and foreshadowing a bleak future of ballooning debt and growing income disparity.

But the averages mask the truly sad story in the Latino population, soon to become California's dominant demographic group. Hispanics attending school in California perform no better than the average student in Mexico, a level comparable to the typical student in Kazakhstan. An alarming 43% of Hispanic students in California did not complete high school between 2005 and 2009, and only 10% attained a college degree.

Anyone worried about income disparity in America should be deeply disturbed. The failure of the K-12 education system for so many students means that issues associated with income distribution—including higher taxes and less freedom in labor and capital markets—will be an ever-present and distressing aspect of our future.

Examples abound of the ability to make sharp improvements in our K-12 system. By not insisting on immediate and widespread reform we are forgoing substantial growth in our standard of living. The problem is obvious. The stakes are enormous. The solutions are within our reach.

Affordable Higher Education Could Be a Great Equalizer

Josh Freedman

Josh Freedman is a policy analyst in the Economic Growth Program at the New America Foundation.

We like to view higher education as the "great equalizer" that leads to social mobility. But selective colleges have long been accused of perpetuating class divides, rather than blurring them.

A Lack of Access to Good Schools

A recent landmark study by Stanford's Caroline Hoxby and Harvard's Christopher Avery lent further empirical evidence to this accusation, finding that high-achieving low-income students do not have access to selective schools. The study showed that the mismatch is due to a lack of knowledge, not quality. Low-income students outside of major urban centers do not even apply to the top-tier colleges for which they are qualified.

Many commentators and the study authors themselves have looked for ways to alleviate this mismatch. A follow-up study found that supplying basic information to applicants could substantially increase the number of low-income students applying to more selective schools. Just giving low-income kids packets of information helped them apply to better schools.

Yet while the information gaps are real and need to be addressed, there is a much deeper structural problem. If most top colleges wanted to be truly equitable, they could not be with their current business model. There is not a golden pot of low-income applicants that schools want but are failing to reach. Instead, many schools don't want more low-income students because they won't be able to pay for them without a major overhaul of school funding practices. Outside of the handful of super-elite universities with fortress endowments, colleges' finances are currently designed around enrolling a disproportionately high number of high-income students. These schools could not afford to support more low-income or middle-income students absent either a huge increase in tuition, a commensurate reduction in spending, or a dramatic change in public funding.

Estimates suggest that 74 percent of students at the 146 top colleges came from the richest quartile of households.

In fact, schools are already moving away from a more equitable system. Colleges actively recruit "full pay" students who can attend and will not need financial aid. A 2011 survey by *Inside Higher Ed* found that about 35 percent of admissions directors at 4-year institutions, particularly public colleges, had increased their efforts to target "full pay" students. Far from wanting to enroll more low-income students, colleges recruit more affluent ones who will pay full price to attend. A follow-up survey of college business officers found that the most common strategy to deal with financial challenges in the next few years was to "raise net tuition revenue." More than 7 in 10 college CFOs [chief financial officers] cited this answer. In other words, schools are becoming more reliant on the inequality in the system than ever before.

If colleges cannot even currently support their business model with enrollment skewed toward higher-income students, a fairer distribution would make the system completely dysfunctional. What's really holding back a more equitable distribution of access to selective colleges is the financial model of colleges. For systemic reform to work, the government will have to take a leading role in fixing incentives and stopping the college spending arms race in its tracks.

The High-Tuition, High-Aid Model

What would selective college populations look like if their student body perfectly reflected the population of qualified students? The short answer is: They would have many more poor students—and it would wreak havoc on their finances.

High-income students account for about a third of the high-achieving students graduating from high school. But estimates suggest that 74 percent of students at the 146 top colleges came from the richest quartile of households. The Center for Education Policy Analysis (CEPA) at Stanford looked at 174 top schools and noted that richest 20 percent of households were seven to eight times more likely to enroll in a selective institution than those from the poorest 20 percent, even though Hoxby and Avery's research suggests that a fairer distribution should be two to one. The CEPA team also found that the gap between the highest and lowest income groups in college enrollment has increased over time, "as more and more seats in highly selective schools have been occupied by students from high income families."

What would the current high-tuition, high-aid model look like with an enrolled student body that reflects the true distribution of high-achieving students?

At The George Washington University [GW], right around the corner from my office in Washington, D.C., the advertised price is $58,985 for the 2012–2013 school year. For the more than 4,000 undergraduate students (out of about 10,000) who are judged to be unable to afford the advertised cost, GW provides an average of $36,789 in aid to offset this cost.

If GW's demographic profile matched the actual distribution of high-achieving students—that is, if there were one bottom-quartile student for every two top-quartile students—

GW's revenue would plummet by about 20 percent. The school would have to raise its tuition for students that are paying full price. But there would be far fewer of them. To take in the same amount of money as they currently do, GW would have to raise its price by approximately $30,000 per full-pay student, for a sticker price of about $90,000 a year. The actual increase would likely need to be more, given that families making $120,000 per year are classified as high income but cannot afford a college cost that would consume three-fourths of their annual income.

This is not a sustainable model. Colleges will not be able to raise sticker prices to these levels while preserving enough aid for low- and middle-income students. They will either raise prices across the board or recruit more affluent students.

Either way, the unequal system will remain.

The Use of Endowments

Not all colleges, however, would need to raise tuition drastically to pay for a larger number of low-income students. Schools with large endowments can cover the shortfall in tuition by drawing money from these reserves. But keeping tuition constant and paying more from the endowment is only an option for schools with monstrous endowments.

Many writers cite Amherst College as a success story, which has [according to The New York Times bureau chief David Leonhardt] "aggressively recruited poor and middle-class students in recent years" and has increased its share of low-income students. But Amherst has a very large endowment for the size of its student body. Its strategy is only viable when backed with an endowment of more than three quarters of a million dollars per student from which it can draw additional funds to cover its costs while remaining competitive in its levels of spending.

Amherst is better than others, however. Some schools that already do have sizable endowments and could increase aid are instead decreasing it. Cornell, which has an endowment of about $5 billion, took $35 million from its endowment in 2009–2010 to fund financial aid. It is now changing its policy to draw less from the endowment, which includes lowering its financial aid policies.

If these trends continue, public universities will limit access to low-income students and increase the number of affluent students.

For GW, with $1.33 billion in its endowment (about 1/18 of Amherst's per student), it's more difficult to use the endowment as a primary backstop. GW only has around 11.7 percent of its endowment, or $155 million, available for student aid. As such, GW—and most selective schools—would only be able to preserve student revenues by raising tuition.

The Public College Crisis

This problem is not reserved for private colleges and universities like GW. In fact, the problem is even worse at public universities.

In addition to competing with private schools, public universities are dealing with cutbacks in public funding as state governments turn to austerity to restore their balance sheets. State funding for colleges and universities dropped substantially after the 2001 and 2008 recessions. States are now spending 28 percent less per college student than they were in 2008, according to the Center on Budget and Policy Priorities, and the College Board reports that average state appropriations for higher education per $1,000 in personal income have declined from $9.74 in 1990 to $5.63 today. These budget cuts have forced states to raise their tuitions in turn. Over just the last 10-year period, combined tuition, fees, and room and board at public 4-year universities have increased 45 percent in inflation-adjusted dollars.

Flagship public universities illustrate this trend. Every flagship state university has seen its tuition increase faster than inflation over the last five years. The biggest price increases are enormous. The University of Arizona raised its tuition 81 percent above inflation, and five other schools saw tuition increases of more than 50 percent in real terms. As one CFO of a public university explained to Andrew Delbanco, the author of *College: What it Was, Is, and Should Be*, the issue at public schools is "not so much the cost of college, but the shift of the financial burden from the state to the student." If these trends continue, public universities will limit access to low-income students and increase the number of affluent students. This will create a more unequal system than the already unequal one we currently have.

Spending on Amenities

All of these calculations assume that colleges do not, and will not, change their spending. But perhaps the key to fixing the structural problem lies on the spending side, rather than the revenue side. Spending is not bad per se. If increased spending is necessary to contribute to the quality of the education or on increased financial aid, it would be good for colleges to continue to spend this money. Unfortunately, much of the spending has been on new buildings, administration, or "amenities" spending, rather than on the education itself.

Financial aid demands will rise for schools that want to attract more low-income students, as David Leonhardt of *The New York Times* notes. He is hopeful that the drive for reputation that includes a commitment to equity and supporting low-income students will encourage colleges to ditch the arms race of spending on new buildings and sports teams. If the spending arms race is a fight for more spending on financial aid, rather than other expenditures, it would be an arms race worth having. He writes:

"It is hard to think of a form of spending more consistent with top colleges' self-image and mission than scholarships for low-income students who have managed to overcome barriers and excel."

The problem, however, is that the capital arms race burnishes a school's reputation far more than a greater commitment to low-income students. Under the current set of incentives, colleges are rewarded for providing more of these "amenities" expenditures but not greater access.

Providing affordable access to more low-income students does not translate into a better reputation.

A recent NBER [National Bureau of Economic Research] working paper found that students value non-instructional amenities and are more likely to attend an institution that spends more on consumption amenities. While high-achieving students also value more spending on instruction (whereas low-achieving students do not, and even think additional instruction is bad), both high-achieving and low-achieving students tend to favor amenities. Universities, responding to this "demand-side pressure," spend more money on these consumption amenities, thus driving up the need for revenue.

Moreover, the current amenities expenditure arms race has succeeded for schools. Before Stephen Joel Trachtenberg took over GW in 1988, the school was "a nonentity in national rankings." Last year it was ranked 51st in the annual *U.S. News & World Report* list. "Spending more money can lead to higher rankings," writes the Center for College Affordability. This perverse incentive encourages the higher spending that leads again to the need for more revenue. Colleges then compete to outspend each other, leading to the never-ending arms race.

Capital Spending and Financial Access

A recent report by my colleague at the New America Foundation, Stephen Burd, tracked colleges' net price for low-income students and what percentage of their students receive federal Pell Grants. Pell Grants can serve as a proxy for how many low-income students are enrolled. Of the 22 selective schools that enrolled a larger share of Pell Grant recipients and kept net price for these students low, only five schools had endowments smaller than $150,000 per student. None of these five schools were ranked in Barron's "most competitive" category. In other words, providing affordable access to more low-income students does not translate into a better reputation. Capital spending of the kind pioneered by GW's Trachtenberg does.

It is difficult to hope that colleges will change their path when the current one they are on has succeeded for their brand, even if it leaves lower- and middle-income students behind.

Perhaps the best example of capital spending trumping financial access is the story of Cooper Union, a small elite private school in New York City that has been free for students since its founding in 1859. Cooper Union used to fund itself on the proceeds from owning the land underneath the Chrysler building and other land assets in New York. To increase its reputation, the school tried to build its brand by building a fancy building. But facing large deficits after taking out a $175 million mortgage to erect the new building and incurring investment losses in the financial crash, the school's board of trustees announced that Cooper Union will start charging undergraduate students tuition in 2014. The consequence of the capital spending, combined with other financial struggles, is that something had to give. Undergraduate students will now be charged tuition (up to about $20,000 per year) for the first time in the school's history.

If reputation cannot slow the spending arms race, could technology? The rise of massively-open online courses, or MOOCs, raises the possibility that we could slash the price of college by replacing expensive college campuses with a broadband connection. But if digital colleges are going to have an effect, it will likely be felt at non-selective low-quality schools, such as for-profits, that currently leave students with few opportunities and plenty of debt. At selective schools, the introduction of online learning does not change the basic incentive structure that pushes schools to spend for the sake of their brand.

It is necessary to have a large public role to guarantee that a basic postsecondary education is not merely a luxury for the wealthy but is instead available, affordably, to every student who wants it.

The Underlying Incentives

In an optimistic scenario, finding ways to increase the information available to high-achieving low-income students would increase the number of applications and put pressure on colleges to end the amenities arms race, decrease costs, and spend more time and resources on learning and education supports.

But a more likely scenario is bleaker. Even if we end the information mismatch, colleges will find ways to preserve their existing business models to avoid fundamental reform. Once again, colleges already do this. Not only do they actively recruit full-pay and out-of-state students, they engage in a practice called "admit-deny." As Burd writes, admit-deny is when "schools deliberately underfund financially needy students in order to discourage them from enrolling." Nearly two-thirds of private colleges and one-third of public schools currently engage in this practice.

We need to fix the underlying incentives, and the best institution to lead these changes is the government. It is necessary to have a large public role to guarantee that a basic postsecondary education is not merely a luxury for the wealthy but is instead available, affordably, to every student who wants it.

A public sector that is not caught up in the arms race should serve as the proper "public option" to attempt to drive down costs at private schools in a semi-competitive sphere. The cutbacks in public funding of higher education have made it more difficult for public institutions to keep their prices down and provide a comparable quality of education. The fact that public schools are actively recruiting full-pay and out of state students means that they are moving away from their necessary function as the core provider of higher education to residents in its state. We need not only to restore funding of public universities, but substantially increase it.

Additionally, many of these schools are reliant on federal aid and federal loan programs to finance their students' educations. For example, the government provides Pell Grants to low-income students up to an amount of $5,550 and subsidizes student loans. Rather than continue to offer federal aid to schools that absorb these costs and continue to operate under the unsustainable high tuition, high-aid model, the government can tie its financial aid support to the elimination of the arms race.

The Need for Government Leverage

As with a military arms race, no individual actor in the education arms race will voluntarily pull back. Only an external force, like the public sector, can make across-the-board changes to fix the problem. The government has leverage because of the importance of federal programs like Pell Grants and subsidized student loans.

To end the arms race, the government should decrease or eliminate federal money to students at schools that continue to increase prices while enrolling disproportionate levels of high income students. Schools would then need to prioritize costs and access, rather than spending and reputation, to be able to function. And no individual school would have to unilaterally draw back.

It is the structural deficiencies in the higher education system that are pushing college further away from being the much-hallowed "great equalizer" and instead perpetuating privilege for those who can pay.

More broadly, the public sector can also help drive down runaway costs by pushing for policies to promote full employment and the creation of good jobs that do not require a college education. When college is all but required to be able to have access to decent quality jobs, colleges can extract economic "rents" because there is no alternative for people entering the labor force. For students who need access to college as an economic stepping-stone to future employment, simultaneous changes on both the educational and labor market fronts can increase the chances of successful reform. Labor market policies to put pressure on college costs can range from creating more useful, high-quality public sector jobs, like childcare and eldercare services, to increasing the minimum wage or supporting workers' bargaining power.

Any and all of these policies will help drive down the natural inclination for colleges to pursue the arms race and push schools back to the quality, accessible education they should be providing.

Until the underlying problems of arms-race expenditures and declining public funding are addressed, colleges will continue to use high-cost, high-aid strategies that are inherently unsustainable and inequitable. Many selective schools derive their status because of the information asymmetry, not in spite of it. It is the structural deficiencies in the higher education system that are pushing college further away from being the much-hallowed "great equalizer" and instead perpetuating privilege for those who can pay.

Education Is Not the Cure for Income Inequality

Lawrence Mishel

Lawrence Mishel is president of the Economic Policy Institute (EPI) and has coauthored eleven editions of The State of Working America, *an ongoing analysis published since 1988 by EPI that provides a wide variety of data on family incomes, wages, jobs, unemployment, wealth, and poverty in the United States.*

With signs pointing to persistent high unemployment and a recovery even weaker than those of the early 1990s and 2000s, it is becoming common to hear in the media and among some policy makers the claim that lingering unemployment is not cyclical but "structural." In this story, the jobs problem is not a lack of demand for workers but rather a mismatch between workers' skills and employers' needs. Another version of the skills mismatch is also being told about the future: we face an impending skills shortage, particularly a shortfall of college graduates, after the economy returns to full employment.

The Purported Solution of Education

The common aspect of each of these claims about structural problems is that education is the solution, the only solution. In other words, delivering the appropriate education and training to workers becomes the primary if not sole policy challenge if we hope to restore full employment in the short and medium term and if we expect to prevent a (further) loss of competitiveness and a further rise in wage and income inequality in the longer term. There are ample reasons to be skeptical of both claims:

- The number of job openings in the current recession has been far too few to accommodate those looking for work, and the shortfall in job openings is pervasive across sectors, not just the hard-hit construction industry, which tends to be the focus of skills-mismatch claims.

- There is no one education group—particularly not the least educated, as the structural argument would suggest—fueling the rise of long-term unemployment in this recession. If there has been some transformation of the workplace leaving millions of workers inadequate for the currently available jobs, then it was not based on a major educational upscaling of jobs.

- The challenge the nation faces as high unemployment persists is not better education and training for those currently unemployed. The problem is a lack of jobs.

- The huge increase in wage and income inequality experienced over the last 30 years is not a reflection of a shortfall in the skills and education of the workforce. Rather, workers face a wage deficit, not a skills deficit. It is hard to find some ever-increasing need for college graduates that is going unmet: college graduates have not seen their real wage rise in 10 years, and the pay gap with high school graduates has not increased in that time period. Moreover, even before the recession college students and graduates were working as free interns, a phenomenon we would not observe if college graduates were in such demand.

In the following I do not present definitive evidence, but I hope to be persuasive enough for readers to demand more evidence before accepting either of these claims of immediate structural employment problems or long-term skills deficits. The first section draws heavily on recent work on structural unemployment in the current recession and, the second draws heavily on the wages chapter of the most recent version of *The State of Working America.*

There has been little evidence offered to support the claim of extensive structural unemployment, and we find that the pattern of employer behavior regarding job openings, layoffs, and hires does not lend it much credence.

The Structural Argument Explaining Unemployment

Unemployment has remained at 9.5% or above since mid-2009 and may remain that high or inch even higher through 2011. The predominant narrative to describe this situation has been that the bursting of the housing and stock bubbles and the financial crisis led to a severe cut-back in household consumption and business investment, causing severe job losses. The policy conclusion drawn from this narrative is that we need faster growth to increase the demand for workers and reduce unemployment.

A competing and, in my view, misguided narrative has also been put forth that a large share of current high unemployment is structural, meaning that those who are unemployed are not well suited to the jobs becoming available. This would be, for instance, because their skills are inadequate, have deteriorated, or are not applicable to the industries that are expanding, or because the unemployed simply do not live where the jobs are. Some make claims about structural unemployment because certain aggregate relationships, such as that between job openings and unemployment, do not appear to be following historical patterns, thereby suggesting a possible skills mismatch. Others have postulated that employers have substantially revamped their production processes in this downturn, thereby eliminating the need for many of the types of workers who are currently unemployed. Still others note that the housing bubble led to a bloated construction sector, and many of those jobs will never come back; displaced construction workers must switch to new jobs for which they may not be qualified. The policy implications of a finding that high unemployment is primarily structural are that: (1) it would be foolhardy to use further demand management (fiscal stimulus, either tax cuts or increased spending, or monetary policy) to lower unemployment, and (2) the appropriate policy is to offer education and training to the unemployed to help them make a transition to new occupations and sectors.

Yet there has been little evidence offered to support the claim of extensive structural unemployment, and we find that the pattern of employer behavior regarding job openings, layoffs, and hires does not lend it much credence. This matters quite a bit for guiding policy. . . .

The Skills Shortage Argument

The second structural issue to examine in the labor market is the claim that the economy faces a looming shortage of college graduates that, if not addressed, will cause flagging competitiveness and further growth in wage and income inequality. A related claim is that the rise in wage inequality over the last 30 years or so can be traced primarily to a technology-driven shift toward a greater need for "more educated" and skilled workers—i.e., college graduates—that was not met by a corresponding increase in the supply of college graduates. This is not necessarily a shortage we face in the next few years, according to some leading economists, but one we will face when the economy returns to full employment.

In response to a question posed by The Economist, "Is America facing an increase in structural unemployment?"

MIT economist Daron Acemoglu wrote an article, "Yes, the labour force hasn't responded to shifting demand for skills." He wrote:

> US structural unemployment is up. But this is not a recent turn of events. It is the continuation of an ongoing process. . . . US employment and demand for labour have been undergoing profound changes over the last 30 years. While the demand for high skill workers, who can perform complex, often non-production tasks, has increased, manufacturing jobs and other "middling occupations" have been in decline. Also noteworthy is that over the last 10–15 years, many relatively low-skill, low-pay service occupations have been expanding rapidly.

David Autor, another MIT economist and a co-author with Acemoglu of important papers on this topic, recently wrote a paper for the Hamilton Project and the Center for American Progress saying:

> Although the U.S. labor market will almost surely rebound from the Great Recession, this paper presents a somewhat disheartening picture of its longer-term evolution. Rising demand for highly educated workers, combined with lagging supply, is contributing to higher levels of earnings inequality. Demand for middle-skill jobs is declining, and consequently, workers that do not obtain postsecondary education face a contracting set of job opportunities.

In reality what the trends mean is that we need more people with advanced degrees, not just college degrees.

The policy implications of this impending skills shortage, according to Autor, are that "an increased supply of college graduates should eventually help to drive down the college wage premium and limit the rise in inequality," and "the United States should foster improvements in K-12 education so that more people will be prepared to go on to higher education." Moreover, we need "training programs to boost skill levels and earnings opportunities in historically low-skilled service jobs—and more broadly, to offer programs for supporting continual learning, retraining, and mobility for all workers." In short, the U.S. needs to create many more college graduates and to provide various types of training for those who do not become college graduates.

The Need for More College Graduates

But the need to *vastly* boost the total number of college graduates in the future may not be as great as Autor and Acemoglu believe. For instance, the trends in the 2000s indicate that the relative demand for college graduates is growing much more slowly than in prior decades. Plus, the wages for college graduates have been flat for about 10 years and running parallel to those with high school degrees, and they have been growing far more slowly than productivity. The implication of these trends is that a surge of college graduates, whatever the benefits (and there are many), can be expected to drive the college wage down. Wage inequality would diminish, but by pressing college graduate wages down (not just in relative terms), which is not the picture frequently painted of the future.

It is important to note that when we discuss the employment or wages of "college graduates" we refer to those with a four-year degree but no further degree; i.e., we exclude both those with advanced or "professional" degrees and those with associate college degrees or with "some college" but no degree past high school. This definition is important because the trends for the aggregate group of all those with a college degree, including those with advanced degrees, is always far more favorable than trends among those with at most a bachelor's degree. For instance, in 2009 the unemployment rate among all college graduates was 4.6%, but those with at most a bachelor's degree had a rate of 5.2% and those with advanced degrees had a rate of 3.4%. There are also very different wage trends among those with only bachelor's degrees (not so good) and those with advanced degrees (much better). And so it is not surprising that analyses which look at the aggregate college group would recommend a vast increase in the supply of college graduates, but in reality what the trends mean is that we need more people with advanced degrees, not just college degrees. It is important to distinguish these groups so we are clear about the findings and implications.

Remarkably, few people seem to know how the workforce breaks down across these categories. . . . About 21% of those employed have at most a bachelors degree, and another 10% have an advanced degree. Only 6.1% of non-immigrant employed workers lack a high school degree (or do not have a GED). A small group, roughly 10%, have an associate's college degree, but an even larger group, about 20%, has attended college but has no degree past high school; this group is labeled "some college."

The Impact of Education

As we have argued in great detail in *The State of Working America* and in other studies dating back to 1994 (with my frequent co-author, Jared Bernstein) technological change and unmet needs for skill have had little to do with the growth of wage inequality over the last 30 years. This is not to say that there hasn't been an increased employer demand for workers with more skills and more education: that has been happening for at least a century. What this means is that the growing need for "education" has been met with a growing supply. For instance, between 1973 and 2007 the share of the workforce with bachelor's degrees and advanced degrees has doubled, from about 10% of the workforce with a bachelor's degree and 4.5% with an advanced degree.

Regardless of the pressures or lack of them from the labor market, it would be a very positive thing to give every student who wants to obtain a college education a real chance—resources and the appropriate education in K-12—to attend *and* complete college, even if this drives down the college wage. One could argue that the issue facing the nation is not so much the need to vastly increase the number of college graduates but to give broader access to the asset of a completed college education. While employer demand is not booming so much that we need to vastly boost college graduation—it will continue to expand at a rate fast enough to satisfy employer needs—it may be the case that moving forward we will have a challenge to generate enough college graduates because we will be exhausting the traditional sources of their supply, the white middle and upper classes.

Most of the growth of wage inequality . . . can be explained by increased wage gaps among workers with the same education . . . than by wage gaps between workers of different educations.

Furthermore, it is still certainly the case that completing college will put a person in a better position in the workplace *relative* to someone who has less education, at least on average. And there are clear non-economic benefits as well, from enjoying better health to being a more informed citizen. Going to college will not be a guarantee of a certain type of income or even access to certain employer benefits—recent college graduates (not just during the recession) earn less in their mid-twenties than those who graduated in the late 1990s, and they are far less likely to have jobs with employer-provided health insurance—yet recent college graduates are clearly faring better than those who have attained only a high school degree. . . .

The Wage Gap

Many media and other discussions of the need for more people to complete college focus on the growth of the college wage premium, that is, the degree to which college graduates earn more than high school graduates. It is frequently assumed, as in the discussion by Autor and Acemoglu above, that the rising college premium accounts for the growth of overall wage inequality. In fact, that is not the case. Most of the growth of wage inequality—the wage gap between a high-wage and low-wage worker—can be explained by increased wage gaps among workers with the same education (e.g., the inequality of wages among college graduates) than by wage gaps between workers of different educations (e.g., the college wage premium). That being the case, then even if greater college enrollment and completion could eliminate the wage gap between college graduates and other workers, much of wage inequality (and the greater extent of wage inequality now versus the past) would still remain, and wage inequality would continue to grow.

In more technical language, there are two dimensions of wage inequality—"between-group" wage differentials, such as those relating to groups defined by their education and experience, and "within-group" wage inequality that occurs among workers of similar education and experience. The growth of within-group inequality can account for roughly 60% of the growth of overall wage inequality since 1973. The connection between growing wage gaps among workers with similar education and experience is not easily related to technological change unless interpreted as a reflection of growing economic returns to worker skills (motivation, aptitudes for math, etc.) that are not easily measured (that is, the regressions used to estimate education differentials cannot estimate these kinds of differentials). However, there are no signs that the growth of within-group wage inequality has been fastest in those industries where the use of technology grew the most. It is also unclear why the economic returns for measurable skills (e.g., education) and unmeasured skills (e.g., motivation) should not grow in tandem. In fact, between-group and within-group inequality have not moved together in the various sub-periods since 1973.

It is surprising that the story of the education premium driving wage inequality persists in the face of its complete failure to explain wage inequality in the 2000s.

The timing of the growth of within-group wage inequality does not easily correspond to the technology story. For instance, consider what happened during the 1995–2000 period associated with a technology-led productivity boom: within-group wage inequality actually declined among women and was essentially flat among men. In the early 1990s, the so-called early stages of the "new economy," within-group wage inequality grew moderately, whereas it grew rapidly in the low-productivity 1980s. Within-group wage inequality did, however, start growing again as productivity accelerated further after 2000 but still lags far behind the 1980s pace. All in all, changes in within-group wage inequality do not seem to mirror the periods of rapid productivity growth or technological change. Perhaps more important, the extent of within-group wage inequality is not affected at all by the supply-side education and training policies that are usually linked to a claim about a shortage of college graduates—so there is no reason to believe that vastly increasing college enrollment and completion will diminish within-group wage inequality.

The growth of inequalities among college graduates has an important practical interpretation as well. As Richard Freeman of Harvard University has pointed out, the wider variance of earnings among college graduates implies that obtaining a college degree is becoming a riskier investment.

The Wages of College Graduates

It is surprising that the story of the education premium driving wage inequality persists in the face of its complete failure to explain wage inequality in the 2000s. Most discussions, like those referred to above, make it seems as if the trends of the 1980s were a juggernaut [unstoppable force] that continued unabated throughout the 1990s and 2000s. In fact, the demand for college graduates relative to other workers has grown the least in this decade compared to other post-war decades, and the college premium, which has grown substantially since the late 1970s, has not grown much at all in recent years. Finally, the actual real wage of college graduates has not grown in about 10 years. Along these lines it is noteworthy that the jobs obtained by young college graduates in recent years pay less than the jobs obtained by those graduating five and 10 years earlier, both in terms of their wages and in the probability that employers provide health insurance or pension coverage.

Together, these trends suggest that the forthcoming supply of college graduates is meeting the growing demands of employers for such workers. Moreover, these trends suggest that a rapid expansion of the supply of college graduates will cause the wages of college graduates to decline, assuming that the productivity-pay gap continues unabated. We can expect the wages of young college graduates and male college graduates (whose wages are currently in decline) to experience the steepest declines. That may or may not be a desirable outcome, but it is definitely not the outcome that most people would expect given the claims that graduating many more people from college will prevent a rise of inequality or reduce inequality.

Higher Education Is Not Always a Smart Monetary Investment

Stephanie Owen and Isabel Sawhill

Stephanie Owen is a senior research assistant and Isabel Sawhill is codirector of the Center on Children and Families at the Brookings Institution.

One way to estimate the value of education is to look at the increase in earnings associated with an additional year of schooling. However, correlation is not causation, and getting at the true causal effect of education on earnings is not so easy. The main problem is one of selection: if the smartest, most motivated people are both more likely to go to college and more likely to be financially successful, then the observed difference in earnings by years of education doesn't measure the true effect of college.

The Monetary Value of a College Degree

Researchers have attempted to get around this problem of causality by employing a number of clever techniques, including, for example, comparing identical twins with different levels of education. The best studies suggest that the return to an additional year of school is around 10 percent. If we apply this 10 percent rate to the median earnings of about $30,000 for a 25- to 34-year-old high school graduate working full time in 2010, this implies that a year of college increases earnings by $3,000, and four years increases them by $12,000. Notice that this amount is less than the raw differences in earnings between high school graduates and bachelor's degree holders of $15,000, but it is in the same ballpark. Similarly, the raw difference between high school graduates and associate's degree holders is about $7,000, but a return of 10% would predict the causal effect of those additional two years to be $6,000.

There are other factors to consider. The cost of college matters as well: the more someone has to pay to attend, the lower the net benefit of attending. Furthermore, we have to factor in the opportunity cost of college, measured as the foregone earnings a student gives up when he or she leaves or delays entering the workforce in order to attend school. Using average earnings for 18- and 19-year-olds and 20- and 21-year-olds with high school degrees (including those working part-time or not at all), Michael Greenstone and Adam Looney of Brookings' Hamilton Project calculate an opportunity cost of $54,000 for a four-year degree.

In this brief, we take a rather narrow view of the value of a college degree, focusing on the earnings premium. However, there are many non-monetary benefits of schooling which are harder to measure but no less important. Research suggests that additional education improves overall wellbeing by affecting things like job satisfaction, health, marriage, parenting, trust, and social interaction. Additionally, there are social benefits to education, such as reduced crime rates and higher political participation. We also do not want to dismiss personal preferences, and we acknowledge that many people derive value from their careers in ways that have nothing to do with money. While beyond the scope of this piece, we do want to point out that these noneconomic factors can change the cost-benefit calculus.

As noted above, the gap in annual earnings between young high school graduates and bachelor's degree holders working full time is $15,000. What's more, the earnings premium associated with a college degree grows over a lifetime. Hamilton

Project research shows that 23- to 25-year-olds with bachelor's degrees make $12,000 more than high school graduates but by age 50, the gap has grown to $46,500. When we look at lifetime earnings—the sum of earnings over a career—the total premium is $570,000 for a bachelor's degree and $170,000 for an associate's degree. Compared to the average up-front cost of four years of college (tuition plus opportunity cost) of $102,000, the Hamilton Project is not alone in arguing that investing in college provides "a tremendous return."

It is always possible to quibble over specific calculations, but it is hard to deny that, on average, the benefits of a college degree far outweigh the costs. The key phrase here is "on average." The purpose of this brief is to highlight the reasons why, for a given individual, the benefits may not outweigh the costs. We emphasize that a 17- or 18-year-old deciding whether and where to go to college should carefully consider his or her own likely path of education and career before committing a considerable amount of time and money to that degree. With tuitions rising faster than family incomes, the typical college student is now more dependent than in the past on loans, creating serious risks for the individual student and perhaps for the system as a whole, should widespread defaults occur in the future. Federal student loans now total close to $1 trillion, larger than credit card debt or auto loans and second only to mortgage debt on household balance sheets.

The Impact of School Selectivity

It is easy to imagine hundreds of dimensions on which college degrees and their payoffs could differ. Ideally, we'd like to be able to look into a crystal ball and know which individual school will give the highest net benefit for a given student with her unique strengths, weaknesses, and interests. Of course, we are not able to do this. What we can do is lay out several key dimensions that seem to significantly affect the return to a college degree. These include school type, school selectivity level, school cost and financial aid, college major, later occupation, and perhaps most importantly, the probability of completing a degree.

Even within a school, the choices a student makes about his or her field of study and later career can have a large impact on what he or she gets out of her degree.

Mark Schneider of the American Enterprise Institute (AEI) and the American Institutes for Research (AIR) used longitudinal data from the Baccalaureate and Beyond survey to calculate lifetime earnings for bachelor's earners by type of institution attended, then compared them to the lifetime earnings of high school graduates. The difference (after accounting for tuition costs and discounting to a present value) is the value of a bachelor's degree. For every type of school (categorized by whether the school was a public institution or a nonprofit private institution and by its selectivity) this value is positive, but it varies widely. People who attended the most selective private schools have a lifetime earnings premium of over $620,000 (in 2012 dollars). For those who attended a minimally selective or open admission private school, the premium is only a third of that. Schneider performed a similar exercise with campus-level data on college graduates (compiled by the online salary information company PayScale), calculating the return on investment (ROI) of a bachelor's degree. These calculations suggest that public schools tend to have higher ROIs than private schools, and more selective schools offer higher returns than less selective ones. Even within a school type and selectivity category, the variation is striking. For example, the average ROI for a competitive public school in 2010 is 9 percent, but the highest rate within this category is 12 percent while the lowest is 6 percent.

Another important element in estimating the ROI on a college education is financial aid, which can change the expected return dramatically. For example, Vassar College is one of the most expensive schools on the 2012 list and has a relatively low annual ROI of 6%. But when you factor in its generous aid packages (nearly 60% of students receive aid, and the average amount is over $30,000), Vassar's annual ROI increases 50%, to a return of 9%.

When we dig even deeper, we see that just as not all college degrees are equal, neither are all high school diplomas.

One of the most important takeaways from the PayScale data is that not every bachelor's degree is a smart investment. After attempting to account for in-state vs. out-of-state tuition, financial aid, graduation rates, years taken to graduate, wage inflation, and selection, nearly two hundred schools on the 2012 list have negative ROIs. Students may want to think twice about attending the Savannah College of Art and Design in Georgia or Jackson State University in Mississippi. The problem is compounded if the students most likely to attend these less selective schools come from disadvantaged families.

The Impact of Field of Study

Even within a school, the choices a student makes about his or her field of study and later career can have a large impact on what he or she gets out of her degree. It is no coincidence that the three schools with the highest 30-year ROIs on the 2012 PayScale list—Harvey Mudd, Caltech, and MIT—specialize in the STEM fields: science, technology, engineering, and math. Recent analysis by the Census Bureau also shows that the lifetime earnings of workers with bachelor's degrees vary widely by college major and occupation. The highest paid major is engineering, followed by computers and math. The lowest paid major, with barely half the lifetime earnings of engineering majors, is education, followed by the arts and psychology. The highest-earning occupation category is architecture and engineering, with computers, math, and management in second place. The lowest-earning occupation for college graduates is service. According to Census's calculations, the lifetime earnings of an education or arts major working in the service sector are actually lower than the average lifetime earnings of a high school graduate.

When we dig even deeper, we see that just as not all college degrees are equal, neither are all high school diplomas. Anthony Carnevale and his colleagues at the Georgetown Center on Education and the Workforce use similar methodology to the Census calculations but disaggregate even further, estimating median lifetime earnings for all education levels by occupation. They find that 14 percent of people with a high school diploma make at least as much as those with a bachelor's degree, and 17 percent of people with a bachelor's degree make more than those with a professional degree. The authors argue that much of this finding is explained by occupation. In every occupation category, more educated workers earn more.

But, for example, someone working in a STEM job with only a high school diploma can expect to make more over a lifetime than someone with a bachelor's degree working in education, community service and arts, sales and office work, health support, blue collar jobs, or personal services. . . .

In fact, choice of major can also affect whether a college graduate can find a job at all. Another recent report from the Georgetown Center on Education and the Workforce breaks down unemployment rates by major for both recent (age 22–26) and experienced (age 30–54) college graduates in 2009–2010. People who majored in education or health have very low unemployment—even though education is one of the lowest-paying majors. Architecture graduates have particularly high unemployment, which may simply reflect the decline of the construction industry during the Great Recession. Arts majors don't fare too well, either. The expected earnings (median full time earnings times the probability of being employed) of a young college graduate with a theater degree are about $6,000 more than the expected earnings of a young high school graduate. For a young person with a mechanical engineering degree, the expected earnings of the college graduate is a staggering $35,000 more than that of a typical high school graduate.

The Importance of Graduating

Comparisons of the return to college by highest degree attained include only people who actually complete college. Students who fail to obtain a degree incur some or all of the costs of a bachelor's degree without the ultimate payoff. This has major implications for inequalities of income and wealth, as the students least likely to graduate—lower-income students—are also the most likely to take on debt to finance their education.

It is a mistake to unilaterally tell young Americans that going to college—any college—is the best decision they can make.

Fewer than 60 percent of students who enter four-year schools finish within six years, and for low-income students it's even worse. Again, the variation in this measure is huge. Just within Washington, D.C., for example, six-year graduation rates range from a near-universal 93 percent at Georgetown University to a dismal 19 percent at the University of D.C. Of course, these are very different institutions, and we might expect high-achieving students at an elite school like Georgetown to have higher completion rates than at a less competitive school like UDC. In fact, Frederick Hess and his colleagues at AEI have documented that the relationship between selectivity and completion is positive, echoing other work that suggests that students are more likely to succeed in and graduate from college when they attend more selective schools. At the most selective schools, 88 percent of students graduate within six years; at non-competitive schools, only 35 percent do. Furthermore, the range of completion rates is negatively correlated with school ranking, meaning the least selective schools have the widest range. For example, one non-competitive school, Arkansas Baptist College, graduates 100 percent of its students, while only 8 percent of students at Southern University at New Orleans finish. Not every student can get into Harvard, where the likelihood of graduating is 97 percent, but students can choose to attend a school with a better track record within their ability level.

Unfortunately, recent evidence by Caroline Hoxby of Stanford and Christopher Avery of Harvard shows that most high-achieving low-income students never even apply to the selective schools that they are qualified to attend—and at which they would be eligible for generous financial aid. There is clearly room for policies that do a better job of matching students to schools.

All of this suggests that it is a mistake to unilaterally tell young Americans that going to college—any college—is the best decision they can make. If they choose wisely and attend a school with generous financial aid and high expected earnings, and if they don't just enroll but graduate, they can greatly improve their lifetime prospects. The information needed to make a wise decision, however, can be difficult to find and hard to interpret.

The Need for Information

One solution is simply to make the type of information discussed above more readily available. A study by Andrew Kelly and Mark Schneider of AEI found that when parents were asked to choose between two similar public universities in their state, giving them information on the schools' graduation rates caused them to prefer the higher-performing school.

The PayScale college rankings are a step in the right direction, giving potential students and their parents information with which to make better decisions. Similarly, the Obama Administration's new College Scorecard is being developed to increase transparency in the college application process. As it operates now, a prospective student can type in a college's name and learn its average net price, graduation rate, loan default rate, and median borrowed amount. The Department of Education is working to add information about the earnings of a given school's graduates. There is also a multi-dimensional search feature that allows users to find schools by location, size, and degrees and majors offered. The Student Right to Know Before You Go Act [in committee as of September 2013], sponsored by Senators Ron Wyden (D-OR) and Marco Rubio (R-FL), also aims to expand the data available on the costs and benefits of individual schools, as well as programs and majors within schools.

Colleges need to do more to ensure that their students graduate, particularly the lower-income students who struggle most with persistence and completion.

The College Scorecard is an admirable effort to help students and parents navigate the complicated process of choosing a college. However, it may not go far enough in improving transparency and helping students make the best possible decisions. A recent report by the Center for American Progress (CAP) showed a draft of the Scorecard to a focus group of college-bound high school students and found, among other things, that they are frequently confused about the term "net price" and give little weight to six-year graduation rates because they expect to graduate in four. It appears that the

White House has responded to some of these critiques, for example showing median amount borrowed and default rates rather than the confusing "student loan repayment." Nevertheless, more information for students and their parents is needed.

There is also room for improvement in the financial aid system, which can seem overwhelmingly complex for families not familiar with the process. Studies have shown that students frequently underestimate how much aid they are eligible for, and don't claim the tax incentives that would save them money. Since 2009, the Administration has worked to simplify the FAFSA [Free Application for Federal Student Aid], the form that families must fill out to receive federal aid—but more could be done to guide low-income families through the process.

In the longer run, colleges need to do more to ensure that their students graduate, particularly the lower-income students who struggle most with persistence and completion. Research suggests that grants and loans increase enrollment but that aid must be tied to performance in order to affect persistence. Currently, we spend over $100 billion on Pell Grants and federal loans, despite a complete lack of evidence that this money leads to higher graduation rates. Good research on programs like Georgia's HOPE scholarships or West Virginia's PROMISE scholarships suggest that attaching strings to grant aid can improve college persistence and completion.

Finally, we want to emphasize that the personal characteristics and skills of each individual are equally important. It may be that for a student with poor grades who is on the fence about enrolling in a four-year program, the most bang-for-the-buck will come from a vocationally oriented associate's degree or career-specific technical training. Indeed, there are many well-paid job openings going unfilled because employers can't find workers with the right skills—skills that young potential workers could learn from training programs, apprenticeships, a vocational certificate, or an associate's degree. Policymakers should encourage these alternatives at the high school as well as the postsecondary level, with a focus on high-demand occupations and high-growth sectors. There has long been resistance to vocational education in American high schools, for fear that "tracking" students reinforces socioeconomic (and racial) stratification and impedes mobility. But if the default for many lower-achieving students was a career-focused training path rather than a path that involves dropping out of traditional college, their job prospects would probably improve. For example, Career Academies are high schools organized around an occupational or industry focus, and have partnerships with local employers and colleges. They have been shown by gold standard research to increase men's wages, hours worked, and employment stability after high school, particularly for those at high risk of dropping out.

In this brief, we have corralled existing research to make the point that while on average the return to college is highly positive, there is a considerable spread in the value of going to college. A bachelor's degree is not a smart investment for every student in every circumstance. We have outlined three important steps policymakers can take to make sure every person does make a smart investment in their choice of postsecondary education. First, we must provide more information in a comprehensible manner. Second, the federal government should lead the way on performance-based scholarships to incentivize college attendance and persistence. Finally, there should be more good alternatives to a traditional academic path, including career and technical education and apprenticeships.

The Wealthy Kids Are All Right

Chuck Collins

Chuck Collins is a senior scholar at the Institute for Policy Studies, where he directs the Program on Inequality and the Common Good.

Two 21-year-old college students sit down in a coffee shop to study for an upcoming test. Behind the counter, a barista whips up their double-shot lattes. In the back kitchen, another young adult washes the dishes and empties the trash.

These four young adults have a lot in common. They are the same age and race, each has two parents, and all grew up in the same metropolitan area. They were all strong students in their respective high schools. But as they enter their third decade, their work futures and life trajectories are radically different—and largely determined at this point.

The culprit is the growing role of inherited advantage, as affluent families make investments that give their children a leg up. Combined with the 2008 economic meltdown and budget cuts in public investments that foster opportunity, we are witnessing accelerating advantages for the wealthy and compounding disadvantages for everyone else.

One of the college students, Miranda, will graduate without any student-loan debt and will have completed three summers of unpaid internships at businesses that will advance her career path. Her parents stand ready to subsidize her lodging with a security deposit and co-signed apartment lease and will give her a no-interest loan to buy a car. They also have a network of family and professional contacts that can help her. While she waits for a job with benefits, she will remain on her parents' health insurance.

Ten years later, Miranda will have a high-paying job, be engaged to another professional, and will buy a home in a neighborhood with other college-educated professionals, a property that will steadily appreciate over time because of its location. The "parental down-payment assistance program" will subsidize the purchase.

The other collegiate, Marcus, will graduate with more than $55,000 in college debt, a maxed-out credit card, and an extensive résumé of part-time food-service jobs that he has taken to pay for school, both during summers and while in college, reducing the hours he can study. Though he will obtain a degree, he will graduate with almost no work experience in his field of study, lose his health insurance, and begin working two part-time jobs to pay back his student loans and to afford rent in a shared apartment.

Ten years later, Marcus will still be working in low-paying jobs and renting an apartment. He will feel occupationally stuck and frustrated in his attempts to network in the area of his degree. He will take on additional debt—to deal with various health and financial problems—and watch his hope of buying a home slip away, in large part because of a credit history damaged during his early twenties.

Tony, the barista, has the benefit of not taking on mega-debt from college. He will eventually enroll in some classes at a local public university. But his income and employment opportunities will be constrained by not having a college degree. He will make several attempts to learn a building trade and start his own business, eventually landing a job with a steady but low income.

The good news for Tony is that his parents, while not college educated or wealthy, are stable middle-class with modest retirement pensions and a debt-free house, acquired by Tony's grandfather with a low-interest Veterans Administration mort-gage. They are able to provide a bedroom to their son. That home will prove to be a significant factor in Tony's future economic stability, as he will eventually inherit it.

[Family wealth] plays an oversize role in sorting today's coming-of-age generation onto different opportunity trajectories.

Cordelia, working in the kitchen, has even less opportunity than Tony for mobility and advancement. Neither of her parents went to college nor have significant assets, as they rent their housing. Though she was academically in the top of her urban high-school class, she did not consider applying to a selective college. The costs seemed daunting, and she didn't know anyone who went away to college. There were no adults or guidance professionals to help her explore other options, including financial aid available at private colleges, some of which would have paid her full tuition and expenses to attend. Instead, she takes courses at the local community college where she sees many familiar faces. Cordelia will struggle with health issues, as lack of adequate health care and insurance means she will delay treatment of several problems. Over time, she will have a steady and low-wage job, but she will also begin to take more responsibility for supporting members of her family who are less fortunate.

The Born-on-Third-Base Factor

These four coming-of-age adults in no way represent the entire spectrum of young adult experience, which also includes ex-offenders, mediocre students, and people with disabilities. Young adults in rural communities and small towns, for example, face their own education and economic challenges, such as limited employment options. They will disproportionately populate our volunteer military, fill the growing ranks of disability-pension recipients, or migrate to communities where they have few social supports.

A key determinant in these diverging prospects is the role of family wealth, a factor that plays an oversize role in sorting today's coming-of-age generation onto different opportunity trajectories. The initial sort begins much earlier. A growing mountain of research chronicles what sociologists call the "intergenerational transmission of advantage," including the myriad mechanisms by which affluent families boost their children's prospects starting at birth. The mechanisms include financial investments in their children's enrichment, school readiness, formal schooling, college access, and aiding the transition to work. Meanwhile, the children in families unable to make these investments fall further behind.

Imagine a ten-mile race in which contestants have different starting lines based on parental education, income, and wealth. The economically privileged athletes start several hundred yards ahead of the disadvantaged runners. Each contestant begins with ten one-pound leg weights. The race begins, and the advantaged competitors pull ahead quickly. At each half-mile mark, according to the rules, the first twenty runners shed two pounds of weights while those in the last half of the field take on two additional pounds. After several miles, lead racers have no weights, while the slower runners carry twenty additional pounds. By midrace, an alarming gap has opened up in the field, and by the finish line, the last half of the field finishes more than two miles behind the winners.

This race of accelerating advantages and compounding disadvantages is a disturbingly accurate metaphor for inherited privilege. As in life, there are well-publicized stories of exceptional runners starting far back in the pack and breaking to the front of the field, therefore able to shed weights and remain competitive. There are also front-runners who perform poorly, squandering their initial advantages and falling back.

But the overall picture is one of steadily growing class-based inequality. Consistent with emerging sociological research about children and opportunity, once inequalities open up, they rarely decrease over time.

A healthy democratic society could rise to this challenge, resolving to make robust public investments in time-tested interventions that equalize the conditions of the race. But in our increasingly plutocratic political system, the very wealthy have less stake in the opportunity-building mechanisms in our communities, as their own children and grandchildren advance through privatized systems. These same wealthy families maintain disproportionate influence in shaping our national priorities, such as whether to cut taxes on the wealthy or maintain investments in public education. We are snagged in a cycle of declining opportunity driven by the new politics of inherited advantage.

The idea that people's futures might be economically determined deeply offends U.S. sensibilities.

A Growing Family Welfare State and a Shrinking Public One

The United States prides itself on being a socially mobile society where what one does is more important than the racial and class circumstances of one's birth. Indeed, in the three decades after World War II, between 1947 and 1977, social mobility increased, particularly for the white working class. This imprinted a national self-identity as a meritocratic society, especially juxtaposed with the old "caste societies" of Europe, with their static class systems and calcified social mobility.

That story of European versus U.S. social mobility has now been turned on its head. European nations and Canada, with their social safety nets and investments in early childhood education, are experiencing greater social mobility.

Canada now has three times the social mobility of the U.S. Budget cuts at all levels of government have dismantled post–World War II public investments that had begun to create greater opportunities for economically and racially disadvantaged families. Higher education has taken one of the biggest hits. Meanwhile, the relative advantage of wealthy families, in terms of social capital and civic engagement, has accelerated over the past 30 years.

The idea that people's futures might be economically determined deeply offends U.S. sensibilities. We want to believe that individual moxie matters, that a person's creativity, effort, and intelligence will lead to economic success. Stories of exceptional strivers, heroically overcoming a stacked deck of obstacles, divert our attention from the data. But the large megatrends are now indisputable. If you fail to pick wealthy parents and want to experience the American dream today, move to Canada.

Parental Investments from Birth

Long before our four 21-year-olds considered college, they were on different glide paths. Debt-free Miranda was the beneficiary of parental investments that prepared her for school and high achievement. She grew up in a book-filled and conversation-rich home environment with college-educated parents that had more leisure and vacation time to spend with her. She spent more time in ecologically pristine environments and had access to recreation, health care, and nutritious food. Her parents, knowledgeable about brain development, talked to her, using vastly more vocabulary words than children of other classes hear. When she was away from her parents, they paid for comparably stimulating child-care settings.

Researcher Meredith Phillips found that by age six, wealthier children spent as many as 1,300 more hours a year than poor children on enrichment activities such as travel, music lessons, visits to museums, and summer camp. All this results in much higher math and reading skills and other attainments later in life.

Success-bound Miranda had more opportunities than her non-wealthy peers to develop the important social capital that results from more time with parents and time spent in social institutions such as religious congregations, civic organizations, and extracurricular activities. Working-class youth, often with parents holding down multiple jobs to make up for several decades of stagnant wages, are more socially disconnected or connected in dysfunctional ways. As a result, they develop fewer "soft skills" useful in job networking and workplaces.

As our foursome enter K-12 school, once considered the great avenue to equal opportunity, disparities widen. The early literacy and reading support conferred by the more advantaged families leads their children to pull away from others, not just those with low incomes. Class-based disparities in the cognitive skills of reading and math test scores have grown since the 1970s, corresponding with the national income and wealth gap. According to researcher Sean Reardon, the income-achievement gap between children from high- and low-income families is roughly 30 percent to 40 percent larger among children born in 2001 than among those born in 1976.

Among "high achievers," the top 4 percent of students nationwide, 34 percent come from the top quartile, households with incomes of more than $120,776. Only 17 percent come from the bottom quartile, with incomes of less than $41,472. The income-achievement gap is now bigger than the race gap, a reverse from 50 years earlier. The main explanation is that high-income parents of all races are investing more in children's cognitive development.

Family Advantage and College Success

All four of our young adults graduated from their high schools in the top fifth of their classes. But their high-school experience was quite divergent, based on their community and neighborhood. The key decision point—as to whether to attend college and where—was largely driven by disparities in income and wealth in the form of parental investment, K-12 education systems, and college-preparatory supports.

In the 70 years since World War II, college attendance has played a significant role in employment opportunity and life-time earnings. Over these 70 years, college entry has increased by more than 50 percent, and the rate of college completion by age 25 has more than quadrupled. But since 1980, an income-based gap has grown up in terms of college completion.

Initial research suggests that financial literacy may be a more important factor than schooling in lifetime wealth accumulation and retirement savings.

Low-income students born around 1980 only increased their college-graduation rates by 4 percent—whereas higher-income cohorts saw their graduation rates go up by 18 percent. The greatest inequality has been among women, driven by increases in college completion by the daughters of higher-income households—and the lack of opportunities for non-wealthy women.

Marcus's family, like Miranda's, placed a strong emphasis on attending college and college preparation. He went to a suburban public school that provided college-bound students with Advanced Placement classes, college counseling, and seminars for parents. While not as wealthy as Miranda's family, Marcus's family, also like Miranda's, paid for the services of the burgeoning college-preparation industry to boost their child's SAT scores. But in terms of family wealth, Marcus was on his own after high school, venturing into higher education and work without family resources and a financial safety net. As a consequence, in his thirties and forties, he will have more debts than assets.

Miranda and barista Tony share an important parental boost that college student Marcus didn't have: Their parents passed on financial-preparation and money-literacy skills. Both children learned about money from parents who gave them allowances to manage and encouraged them to open bank accounts and save. Initial research suggests that financial literacy may be a more important factor than schooling in lifetime wealth accumulation and retirement savings. Tony learned thrift and debt avoidance. These skills are much more important in the current environment, with unregulated predatory lenders and a bewildering variety of student-loan products to choose from.

Tony will benefit from modest family-wealth transfers, thanks to a previous generation of social investments, which include his grandfather's government-subsidized home mortgage. Tony will tap into what Sally Koslow, in her book *Slouching toward Adulthood*, calls the "middle class trust fund": free room and board and cable and Internet access. Tony's parents don't consider their support for him a legacy advantage. They understand that the deck is stacked against their son, who will most likely never be rich without a winning lottery ticket or marrying into money. Their temporary housing and modest gifts—the purchase of a truck and money to get a trade license—are hedges against his downward mobility and destitution.

Cordelia's parents did what they could to better her prospects, ensuring she was in a good elementary school and steered to engaging teachers. They found her affordable summer day camps and other enrichment experiences. But when it came time for her to consider college, Cordelia was flying solo. Like many talented low-income students, she didn't apply to one of the nation's selective schools. Only 5 percent of the total enrollment at the 28 most selective private colleges is from families in the bottom fifth of income distribution. But 70 percent of the enrollment consists of students in the highest-income distribution. Like the majority of low-income college students, Cordelia did not complete college. A key missing ingredient for Cordelia was effective college guidance, within her school and at home.

Young adults may make poor decisions or face unforeseen circumstances, but in almost every case, family wealth will help keep young people on track.

How young people finance college has its own disparities. Low-income and minority students that get proper guidance can sometimes obtain significant scholarships at private colleges and graduate with less debt than students attending public universities. Miranda's parents paid full freight for her college. Marcus, navigating the college-financing jungle on his own, got little financial aid and signed up for a loan package that will cost him twice as much over time due to higher interest payments as the cheapest available plan. If Marcus were attending college 40 years earlier, he probably would have graduated debt-free as a result of lower tuition and public financial-aid programs.

One of the huge breakaway wealth advantages is unpaid internships in one's career area, an essential leg up in the transition from school to work. Entry-level workers are now expected to show up with work experience. Research shows that half of college-graduate hires had previously interned at the firm where they were hired. While Miranda received family support to take unpaid internships, other college students like Marcus used every non-school hour to earn money in jobs outside their career area.

Family wealth also serves as a form of adversity insurance, as young adults face potential setbacks including prolonged unemployment, bad credit, health or addiction problems, criminal arrests, car breakdowns or accidents, or early parenthood. Young adults may make poor decisions or face unforeseen circumstances, but in almost every case, family wealth will help keep young people on track, whether it comes in legal assistance, treatment, or regular cash infusions.

Closing the Advantage Gap

What, if anything, can be done to offset the torrent of perks and advantages that wealthy parents confer to their progeny as they compete for slots in educational institutions, internships in their field of interest, entry-level jobs, affordable housing, and other resources?

The first step is to acknowledge the depth of the declining mobility and opportunity problem, a story that is just beginning to be understood after three decades of extreme inequality. The image of post–World War II white mobility still reverberates and dominates our national mythology, especially for our political class and whites over the age of 50. But the present inequalities of wealth have fundamentally altered the playing field for the next two generations.

> *The fact that inequalities of opportunity now accelerate as schooling begins is testament to the need to defend and expand funding for public education at all levels.*

Even ideological critics of social investment have begun to acknowledge the intergenerational class disparities. Conservative Reihan Salam acknowledges the "incumbent-protection story" of wealthy families, observing that "it is possible that non-black families in the top three-fifths of the income distribution are giving their children advantages that protect them from scrappy upstarts in ways that might damage our growth prospects." Let alone principles of fairness, opportunity, and equity!

Sustained public investments in opportunity are critical to level a playing field that is constantly being upended by wealth advantage. We can't remove the capacity of well-off families to help advantage their offspring, but we can give others more of a shot.

Other industrialized countries have demonstrated that public investments in health, education, and family well-being can offset the private advantages of wealth and improve social mobility. Initiatives like the "Baby College" of the Harlem Children's Zone, Head Start, the U.S.'s Nurse-Family Partnership program, and universal preschool programs, such as those in France and Denmark, partially close the gaps in school achievement and subsequent wages. Several of these initiatives coach new parents on childhood health and wellness, discipline, brain development, and games and enrichment resources available to their children.

High-quality pre-kindergarten education, access to health care and nutrition, good K-12 public education, and early diagnosis of learning disabilities and special needs are key interventions that help people equalize life chances. The fact that inequalities of opportunity now accelerate as schooling begins is testament to the need to defend and expand funding for public education at all levels. More than three-fourths of undergraduate college students attend public universities and colleges, which are facing the worst state cuts.

There are also private-sector and personal interventions that could reduce runaway unequal opportunity. Community foundations can partner with business and cultural institutions to ensure that public and private funding for youth enrichment, arts and sports programs, summer camps, and stimulating after-school programs survive budget cutting. This must include resources for outreach to the most socially disconnected families to ensure their children have access to these opportunities.

The U.S. Department of Labor should police the unpaid and underpaid internship marketplace, cracking down on companies that replace paid positions with unpaid ones. Certain sectors that disproportionately offer unpaid internships as a stepping-stone to career networks—journalism, politics, and entertainment—should do deep soul-searching about the implications for the widespread exclusion of working- and middle-class youth. Private-sector and government agencies that offer internships should create stipend and compensation pools to ensure that non-wealthy young people have an equal shot at internships. Donors should fund internship positions at nonprofit organizations they care about, expanding the pool of young people that can intern there.

Privileged families will always seek to extend their own advantages to their children, but restoring greater progressivity to the tax system would ensure that wealthy families still contribute to the opportunities of others. Another intervention would be to eliminate or reduce the tax deductibility of contributions to private schools and colleges, except if directly used for scholarships for disadvantaged youth.

One elegant solution would be to tax wealth to broaden opportunity. Revenue from a steeply progressive estate or inheritance tax could capitalize an "education-opportunity trust fund" to provide debt-free college educations for first-generation college students.

Wealthy families concerned about declining social mobility should use their special privileges to stop the advantage arms race. They should match any family subsidies with tax dollars and donations to organizations that promote mobility. Without such interventions, the U.S. will further drift toward being a caste society, where opportunity, occupation, and social status are based on inherited advantage, fractured along class lines.

Organizations to Contact

The editors have compiled the following list of organizations concerned with the issues debated in this book. The descriptions are derived from materials provided by the organizations. All have publications or information available for interested readers. The list was compiled on the date of publication of the present volume; names, addresses, phone and fax numbers, and e-mail and Internet addresses may change. Be aware that many organizations take several weeks or longer to respond to inquiries, so allow as much time as possible.

American Association of University Women (AAUW)
1111 Sixteenth St. NW, Washington, DC 20036
(800) 326-2289 • fax: (202) 872-1425
e-mail: helpline@aauw.org
website: www.aauw.org

The American Association of University Women (AAUW) promotes equity and education for women and girls. Through advocacy, education, and research AAUW aims to support women in their careers and promote pay equity. AAUW publishes numerous reports dealing with issues of wage and gender, including "The Simple Truth About the Gender Pay Gap."

American Enterprise Institute (AEI)
1150 17th St. NW, Washington, DC 20036
(202) 862-5800 • fax: (202) 862-7177
e-mail: info@aei.org
website: www.aei.org

The American Enterprise Institute (AEI) is a private, nonpartisan, and nonprofit institution dedicated to research and education on issues of government, politics, economics, and social welfare. AEI sponsors research and publishes materials aimed at defending the principles, and improving the institutions, of American freedom and democratic capitalism. Among AEI's publications is the online magazine, *The American*.

American Federation of Labor and Congress of Industrial Organizations (AFL-CIO)

815 16th St. NW, Washington, DC 20006
(202) 637-5000
website: www.aflcio.org

The American Federation of Labor and Congress of Industrial Organizations (AFL-CIO) is a voluntary federation of fifty-six national and international labor unions, representing 12.2 million members. The AFL-CIO educates union members about issues that affect the daily lives of working families and encourages them to make their voice heard by government. The AFL-CIO has numerous publications available at its website, including "CEO Pay and You."

Center for American Progress (CAP)

1333 H St. NW, 10th Floor, Washington, DC 20005
(202) 682-1611 • fax: (202) 682-1867
website: www.americanprogress.org

The Center for American Progress (CAP) is a nonprofit, nonpartisan organization dedicated to improving the lives of Americans through progressive ideas and action. CAP dialogues with leaders, thinkers, and citizens to explore the vital issues facing America and the world. The organization publishes numerous research papers, which are available at its website, including "What Causes the Gender Wage Gap?"

Center for Economic and Policy Research (CEPR)

1611 Connecticut Ave. NW, Suite 400, Washington, DC 20009
(202) 293-5380 • fax: (202) 588-1356
e-mail: cepr@cepr.net
website: www.cepr.net

The Center for Economic and Policy Research (CEPR) aims to promote democratic debate on the most important economic and social issues that affect people's lives. CEPR conducts both professional research and public education. CEPR provides briefings and testimony to Congress and reports for the general public, including "Inequality as Policy: The United States Since 1979."

Center on Budget and Policy Priorities (CBPP)
820 First St. NE, Suite 510, Washington, DC   20002
(202) 408-1080 • fax: (202) 408-1056
e-mail: center@cbpp.org
website: www.cbpp.org

The Center on Budget and Policy Priorities (CBPP) is a policy organization working at the federal and state levels on fiscal policy and public programs that affect low- and moderate-income families and individuals. CBPP conducts research and analysis to inform public debates over proposed budget and tax policies, developing policy options to alleviate poverty. There are many reports available at CBPP's website, including "Pulling Apart: A State-by-State Analysis of Income Trends."

Economic Policy Institute (EPI)
1333 H St. NW, Suite 300, East Tower, Washington, DC   20005
(202) 775-8810 • fax: (202) 775-0819
e-mail: epi@epi.org
website: www.epi.org

The Economic Policy Institute (EPI) is a nonprofit think tank that seeks to broaden the discussion about economic policy to include the interests of low- and middle-income workers. EPI briefs policy makers at all levels of government; provides technical support to national, state, and local activists and community organizations; testifies before national, state, and local legislatures; and provides information and background to the print and electronic media. EPI publishes books, studies, issue briefs, popular education materials, and other publications, among which is its flagship publication, *The State of Working America*, the full text of which is available online.

Institute for Women's Policy Research (IWPR)
1200 18th St. NW, Suite 301, Washington, DC   20036

(202) 785-5100 • fax: (202) 833-4362
e-mail: iwpr@iwpr.org
website: www.iwpr.org

The Institute for Women's Policy Research (IWPR) conducts research and disseminates its findings to address the needs of women, promote public dialog, and strengthen families, communities, and societies. With initiatives on the topics of education, democracy, poverty, work, and health, IWPR aims to promote gender equity. IWPR publishes numerous reports and briefing papers, including "Pay Secrecy and Wage Discrimination."

United for a Fair Economy (UFE)

1 Milk St., 5th Floor, Boston, MA   02109
(617) 423-2148 • fax: (617) 423-0191
e-mail: info@faireconomy.org
website: www.faireconomy.org

United for a Fair Economy (UFE) aims to raise awareness that concentrated wealth and power undermine the economy, corrupt democracy, deepen the racial divide, and tear communities apart. UFE supports and helps build social movements for greater equality through such projects as its Racial Wealth Divide program. UFE has numerous resources available at its website, including reports and infographics.

Urban Institute

2100 M St. NW, Washington, DC   20037
(202) 833-7200
website: www.urban.org

The Urban Institute works to foster sound public policy and effective government by gathering data, conducting research, evaluating programs, and educating Americans on social and economic issues. The Urban Institute builds knowledge about the nation's social and fiscal challenges through evidence-based research meant to diagnose problems and figure out which policies and programs work best, for whom, and how.

The Institute publishes policy briefs, commentary, and research reports, including "Risk and Recovery: Understanding the Changing Risks to Family Incomes."

Bibliography

Books

Orazio P. Attanasio, Erich Battistin, and Mario Padula — *Inequality in Living Standards Since 1980*. Washington, DC: AEI Press, 2010.

Francine D. Blau — *Gender, Inequality, and Wages*. New York: Oxford University Press, 2012.

Jim Clifton — *The Coming Jobs War: What Every Leader Must Know About the Future of Job Creation*. New York: Gallup Press, 2011.

Chuck Collins — *99 to 1: How Wealth Inequality Is Wrecking the World and What We Can Do About It*. San Francisco: Berrett-Koehler Publishers, 2012.

Uri Dadush et al. — *Inequality in America*. Washington, DC: Brookings Institution Press, 2012.

Peter Edelman — *So Rich, So Poor: Why It's So Hard to End Poverty in America*. New York: New Press, 2012.

Diana Furchtgott-Roth — *Women's Figures: An Illustrated Guide to the Economic Progress of Women in America*. Washington, DC: AEI Press, 2012.

Lilly Ledbetter and Lanier Scott Isom — *Grace and Grit: My Fight for Equal Pay and Fairness at Goodyear and Beyond*. New York: Crown Archetype, 2012.

Leslie McCall — *The Undeserving Rich: American Beliefs about Inequality, Opportunity, and Redistribution*. New York: Cambridge University Press, 2013.

Timothy Noah — *The Great Divergence: America's Growing Inequality Crisis and What We Can Do About It*. New York: Bloomsbury Press, 2012.

June O'Neill and Dave O'Neill — *The Declining Importance of Race and Gender in the Labor Market: The Role of Federal Employment Policies*. Washington, DC: AEI Press, 2012.

Benjamin I. Page and Lawrence R. Jacobs — *Class War? What Americans Really Think About Economic Inequality*. Chicago: University of Chicago Press, 2009.

Robert B. Reich — *Aftershock: The Next Economy and America's Future*. New York: Vintage Books, 2011.

Tavis Smiley and Cornel West — *The Rich and the Rest of Us: A Poverty Manifesto*. New York: Smiley Books, 2012.

Joseph Stiglitz — *The Price of Inequality: How Today's Divided Society Endangers Our Future*. New York: W.W. Norton, 2012.

Periodicals and Internet Sources

Jamelle Bouie
"The Titanic Wealth Gap Between Blacks and Whites," *American Prospect*, February 27, 2013. www.prospect.org.

Ronald Brownstein
"A Broken Ladder," *National Journal*, March 9, 2013.

Bureau of Labor Statistics, US Department of Labor
"Women in the Labor Force: A Databook," Report 1034, December 2011. www.bls.gov.

Steve Conover
"The Myth of Middle-Class Stagnation," *American*, September 16, 2011. www.american.com.

Bryce Covert
"The Inescapable Gender Wage Gap," *Nation*, October 24, 2012. www .nation.com.

Dave Gilson and Carolyn Perot
"It's the Inequality, Stupid," *Mother Jones*, March/April 2011.

Michael Greenstone and Adam Looney
"The Uncomfortable Truth About American Wages," *Economix*, October 22, 2012. www.economix.blogs .nytimes.com.

Ron Haskins
"The Myth of the Disappearing Middle Class," *Washington Post*, March 29, 2012.

Ariane Hegewisch, Claudia Williams, and Angela Edwards — "The Gender Wage Gap: 2012," Institute for Women's Policy Research, March 2013. www.iwpr.org.

Steven Horwitz — "Markets and the Gender Wage Gap: Are Employers Sexist?" *Freeman*, March 17, 2011. www.fee.org/the_freeman.

Richard W. Johnson and Janice S. Park — "Employment and Earnings Among 50 l People of Color," Urban Institute, August 2011. www.urban.org.

Daniel Kuehn — "The Labor Market Performance of Young Black Men in the Great Recession," Urban Institute, February 2013. www.urban.org.

Steven J. Markovich — "The Income Inequality Debate," Council on Foreign Relations, September 2012. www.cfr.org.

Aparna Mathur and Michael R. Strain — "Are Minimum Wages Fair?" *Blaze*, July 18, 2012. www.theblaze.com.

Marla McDaniel and Daniel Kuehn — "What Does a High School Diploma Get You? Employment, Race, and the Transition to Adulthood," *Review of Black Political Economy*, October 2012.

Ryan Messmore — "Justice, Inequality, and the Poor," *National Affairs*, Winter 2012.

Charles Murray — "The New American Divide," *Wall Street Journal*, January 23, 2012.

Amani M. Nuru-Jeter and Thomas A. LaVeist — "Racial Segregation, Income Inequality, and Mortality in US Metropolitan Areas," *Journal of Urban Health*, April 2011.

June E. O'Neill — "The Disappearing Gender Wage Gap," National Center for Policy Analysis, June 22, 2012. www.ncpa.org.

Pew Charitable Trusts — "Income and Wealth in America Across Generations," Economic Mobility Project, February 2013. www.pewstates.org.

Jonathan Rauch — "Inequality and Its Perils," *National Journal*, September 27, 2012. www.nationaljournal.com.

John Schmitt — "The Minimum Wage Is Too Damn Low," Center for Economic and Policy Research, March 2012. www.cepr.net.

Nick Schulz — "Raising Minimum Wage Is Maximum Stupidity," *Boston Herald*, April 11, 2012.

Christina Hoff Sommers — "The Equal Pay Day Reality Check," *American*, April 20, 2010. www.american.com.

Thomas J. Sugrue — "A House Divided," *Washington Monthly*, January/February 2013.

Derek Thompson   "The Biggest Myth About the Gender
                   Wage Gap," *Atlantic*, May 30, 2013.
                   www.theatlantic.com.

Christian E.   "The State of Communities of Color
Weller, Julie   in the US Economy: Still Feeling the
Ajinkya, and Jane Pain Three Years into the Recovery,"
Farrell   Center for American Progress, April
                   2012. www.americanprogress.org.

Will Wilkinson   "Thinking Clearly About Economic
                   Inequality," Cato Institute, July 14,
                   2009. www.cato.org.

James Q. Wilson   "Angry About Inequality? Don't
                   Blame the Rich," *Washington Post*,
                   January 26, 2012.

Scott Winship   "Inequality Is Not What We
                   Imagine," *New York Times*, October
                   19, 2012.

Index